The 20th Century Capitalist Revolution

Adolf A. Berle, Jr., born in Boston and educated at Harvard University, is a practicing lawyer. Since 1928 he has taught at Columbia University, where he is Professor Emeritus of Law and a member of the Political Science Faculty, and since 1954 has lectured at the United States Air War College. He has received honorary degrees from the University of Brazil; the University of the Andes, Colombia; Queens University, Canada; Oberlin College, Ohio; and Yankton College, South Dakota.

During his distinguished career of public service, Mr. Berle has held numerous public offices, including those of Treasurer of the City of New York from 1934 to 1938, Assistant Secretary of State of the United States from 1938 to 1944, and Ambassador to Brazil from 1945 to 1946. In 1960 he served as Chairman of President Kennedy's Task Force on Latin American policy, and in 1961 as Special Assistant to the Secretary of State. He is presently Chairman of the Board of The Twentieth Century Fund.

Mr. Berle is the author of, among other books, *The Modern Corporation and Private Property* (with Dr. G. C. Means), *Tides of Crisis, Power Without Property, Latin America: Diplomacy and Reality,* and *The American Economic Republic.*

ADOLF A. BERLE, JR.

The 20th Century Capitalist Revolution

———

HARCOURT, BRACE & WORLD, INC.

NEW YORK

FOREWORD

The genesis of this study was an invitation by the Faculty of the Northwestern University School of Law to give a series of lectures under the auspices of the Julius Rosenthal Foundation. The book here presented is based on, and an expansion of, The Rosenthal Lectures of 1954. It had been decided that a subject connected with modern corporation law might be interesting. Under the kindly guidance of Dean Havighurst, however, it was decided to attempt studying the modern corporation from a novel angle.

Corporations have been analyzed as legal entities for generations. Some thirty years ago a new approach was attempted: they were dealt with as economic institutions. The time seemed to have come to study them now as quasi-political institutions as well. The study thus comes to be more a study in the field of political science than in that of technical law.

From the point of view of a Law School Faculty, and of a legal study foundation like that set up in memory of Julius Rosenthal, this was a controversial innovation. But the Faculty of the Northwestern University School of Law were in no way embarrassed by that. Modern law concerns itself with institutions quite as much as with rules. Here is a new, and typical, American institution, pushing itself into the field of statecraft as well as of commercial law. It

5

has become in fact a major agency by which the economic life of the United States is carried on. Almost involuntarily it has become a factor in the organizational life of the most productive republic in the world. Probably old Julius Rosenthal himself, who immigrated to the United States after the German Revolution of 1848 and was a mighty figure at the Chicago Bar when the American industrial system was forming itself, would, I think, have been the first to recognize that political science and law are as intimately connected in the America of the twentieth century as they were in the Europe of the nineteenth.

I owe many debts of gratitude in connection with this modest offering, which I hope may be the forerunner of a more substantial study to come. First, my thanks go to my students in the Columbia Law School Seminar on Advanced Corporation Problems. For some years these young men and women have worked on various aspects of the problem which this book indicates rather than describes. To three men now dead, I must pay a tribute of grateful humility and recognition: to Professor William Z. Ripley of Harvard; to Professor Huger W. Jervey and to Professor Wesley Clair Mitchell, both of Columbia. Ripley was an anthropologist turned economist. Jervey was a great legal scholar. Mitchell pioneered the entire subject of institutional economics. All three encouraged me to follow the line of study of which this book is one product.

Recognition must also be given to Miss Margaret Poole who struggled with the manuscript in various drafts, often amid my own distraction by other, more violent though perhaps less fruitful, adventures.

ADOLF A. BERLE, JR.

Columbia University,
New York City, 1954.

CONTENTS

I

The Modern Corporation and the
Capitalist Revolution

This is a study of one aspect of the revolutionary capitalism of the mid-twentieth century. The staging area is the study of certain results of the modern corporation. This singular organization has succeeded in being at once legal institution, economic institution, and agency and chief heir of the explosion of technical progress which is the outstanding achievement of our generation.

No adequate study of twentieth-century capitalism exists. Scholarly commentators are quite aware that the descriptive clichés still in current use are little more than a deposit of verbiage left over from a previous historical age.

When, in 1859, the Emperor Napoleon III made war on Austria, he is said to have consulted Jomini, an aging Marshal of the time of the great Napoleon. Jomini planned the campaign along lines of the hallowed tradition of 1809. But as Mr. Philip Guedalla

9

acidly observed, you could never beat the Austrians at that. To a campaign begun in 1859 but prosecuted with the ideas of 1809, the Austrian Empire unerringly opposed the strategic concepts of 1759. Naturally the French won the war. Somewhat the same observation could be made concerning the attacks on American twentieth-century capitalism, and the defenses raised by it. The attacks stem from a long current of social thought in Europe culminating in the theories of Karl Marx (approximately 1870), repeated with wearying iteration by Communist philosophers today. In reply the principal defenders of capitalism have reiterated theories and descriptions of capitalism propounded by Adam Smith in 1776, developed to a high point by Ricardo in 1817. No one, it seems, has seriously undertaken to restate the actual practice of American capitalism as it has developed since, let us say, 1930, describing its operations and results, and readjusting theories to conform to fact. In large measure, indeed, the defense has been left to journalists and public relations experts while businessmen stood mute. The real business of American capitalism should have been the staging of a solid counterattack.

This it has every right to do. Its aggregate economic achievement is unsurpassed. Taking all elements (including human freedom) into account, its system of distributing benefits, though anything but perfect, has nevertheless left every other system in recorded history immeasurably far behind. Its rate of progress shows no sign of slackening. Even its instabilities and crises relied on by Marx and by the present Soviet government to destroy its surrounding social fabric show indications of becoming manageable—and certainly they are more manageable than the political instabilities and crises instinct in any competing system. All the materials for a crushing counterargument are present.

But they cannot be marshaled without modifying the ideological lines of yesterday. For this reason, the ensuing study discards, and occasionally treats disrespectfully, some of the hallowed phrases dear to lawyers, economists, businessmen, and the advertising fraternity. It is simply inaccurate to present the American corporate system of 1954 as a system in which competition of great units (which does exist) produces the same results as those which used to flow from competition among thousands of small producers (which in great areas of American economics in the main does not exist). It is plainly contrary to fact to represent that the great collective enterprise known as a corporation follows a course similar to the limited private enterprise of Ricardo's individual entrepreneur. It is merely misleading to present the vast operations of corporate concentrates as "private"—except in the sense that they are not statist, and even that is subject to some qualification as will later appear. Even the classic law of supply and demand requires a second look in an economic system which does its level best, frequently with success, in creating a planned equation of supply to demand such as is practiced in the oil industry and the sugar industry. And it is indefensibly disingenuous to assert that these operations are primarily following economic laws more or less accurately outlined by the classic economists a century ago when the fact appears to be that they are following a slowly emerging pattern of sociological and political laws, relevant to the rather different community demands of our time.

We shall, I am afraid, sketch a picture considerably removed from the character of American business and the American economic system which stalks the financial pages of many newspapers. We shall find instead a far more effective, far more sensitive, and (to the writer) a far more appealing organization of affairs than ever was described under the aegis of *laissez faire*. With its successes, come failures; with its values, defects; with its great possibilities, great dangers; in fact, great adventures in a new age are in the making.

2

The first half of the twentieth century presented the West with an interesting paradox. The period has been fertile and bold beyond belief in producing hypotheses in physical science. It has produced no correspondingly great hypothesis in the field of economics or in politics. Physical science has been carried through experimentation to practical application, and the face of the world has been changed. But in economics we are only beginning to accumulate the measurements and tools upon which scientific theories may later be constructed. In politics we are frankly traveling on intuition except where we follow theoretical ideas propounded by economists and philosophers of whom perhaps the latest are Karl Marx who died in 1883 and Heinrich von Treitschke who died in 1896.

The contrasting results of this disparity are sufficiently striking. Medical science has apparently made it possible to change population trends appreciably in whole nations (including the United States) as application of its developments widened. Physical science under the leadership of Einstein and Nils Bohr has superimposed a new world upon the old—a world including atomic destruction and possible creation, unplumbed possibilities of electronics, and unexplored but clearly possible variations of matter and material. Material conditions of life are rapidly changing to the point of incredibility. If a group of men meeting in 1910 had stated their intention to transform the United States through use of the combustion engine into an auto-mobile-borne, airborne country, and to revolutionize housing, commerce, agriculture, transportation, and the structure of cities to match, they would perhaps have been prosecuted as subversive, or more probably classi-fied as lunatics. Yet precisely this happened in a span of thirty years. If at the same time a group of doctors had pronounced that they would so alter medical and public health techniques that the world could fight two planetary wars yet consistently increase the popu-lation of the chief belligerents during both, they would have been heard with attention but with incredulity. If they had added that they could aid in changing the rate of population increase in the United States so as to promise a population of 160 million by the year 1953, incredulity would probably have been accom-panied by concern. Had the agricultural botanists added that they could so increase food production that, arrived at this figure, the food problem would be that of taking care of farm surplus instead of running a losing race with demand, only the sophisticated would have troubled to pay much heed. These things all have

14

happened. In mid-century, it seems probable they pre-
sage more sweeping changes still to come.

Meanwhile in the category of social sciences, lacking
an equivalent base of pioneer abstract theory, most of
the world is proceeding empirically. Methods of economic engineering are roughly the same as those prevailing during World War I when reserve banking became general throughout the western world. Methods
of international politics would even seem to have re-
ceded to a level far below those prevailing in the nineteenth century; the history of relations between nations
in many respects rivals the terrible chronicles of the
wars of the Reformation in the sixteenth and seven-
teenth centuries. Political organization of states and the
power within them has, I think, made advances; but the
advances have been attained through trial and error or
accidental discovery rather than through application
of theoretical analysis.

This justifies a not inconsiderable concern. It is reasonable to suppose that the rapid increase of technical
advance, and (if the recent estimates of Dr. W. S.
Woytinsky are justified) an increase in the population
of the world by 850 million in the next fifty years (not
to mention probable increase of the population of the
United States in the same period to probably more than
200 million), will, of necessity, impose a vastly greater

strain on our ability to organize and to govern. It is true that technical advance, past and prospective, justifies the assumption that there will be adequate supplies of food, shelter and so forth, to satisfy wants. But the task of organizing and distributing them will vastly increase. Finally, since human beings are not insects, preservation of their individuality and dignity within this accelerated system becomes a matter of first importance. All this falls within the realm of what the Greeks called "politics," or what we call, with loose inadequacy today, the "field of social science." But this science is still a dream; the very name expresses a hope rather than describes a reality.

The default of the twentieth century in this field appears not to have been adequately explained. Perhaps a fair guess is that lack of bold theory left political science without any accepted working hypothesis, and by consequence without any method of effective observation of phenomena. For unless there is some hypothesis (whatever its later fate) there is no basis for selecting the phenomena which should be observed, and no means of describing them so that descriptions can become the basis for classification; and consequently no way of relating them so that a sequence of acts and effect may be tolerably established. In result, no principles can be derived which make it possible to apply to the decisions of tomorrow deductions from the experience of yesterday. Even a bad hypothesis organizes thinking and observation sufficiently to permit determination that the hypothesis is wrong. No hypothesis at all produces an aimless collection of data somewhat like Sir W. S. Gilbert's "Interesting Facts about the Square of the Hypotenuse"—except, of course, that we know a good deal about a hypotenuse, and very little about human organization.

This prelude is the justification for tackling one of the reasonably definite and observable phenomena—the large American corporation—as a study in politics. Corporations are organizations of human beings. Their history and results are in broad limit ascertainable. The laws under which they operate are in the main conventional. Their statistical impact on at least the American economy is beginning to be charted. Their importance in the American state is obvious, whether considered as means of production, instruments of distribution, sources of occupation, or agents of economic progress. Perhaps it will not be disputed (though data will be later given) that they have been essentially revolutionary instruments in twentieth-century capitalism; that, indeed, they have been one cause, if not the major cause, of its evolution to a state undreamed of in earlier economic theory. They can accordingly be profitably studied. The study may perhaps assist in pointing toward at least the possibility of a solidly based twentieth-century political hypothesis.

3

Legalistics aside, any large corporation is first and foremost an institution. If by an act of the state, court decision, or in some other fashion, it were suddenly deprived of its supposed legal existence—say, if its charter were canceled—a moment of astonishment might affect the minds of its directors, officers, employees, customers, creditors, and so forth. But one imagines that the instantaneous reaction would be one of mild amusement—like that pictured in a famous cartoon showing a workman at the top of a vast dam bellowing through a microphone to a workman at the bottom of it that the dam had been declared unconstitutional. The dam would still be there—and so would the corporation. Clearly it is not the law, with its fiction of juristic personality, that supplies the life blood and beating heart of these vast mechanisms. If the law, acting through some instrumentality, declared that they did not exist, the entities would be found to be not fictitious, but factual. The railroad would go right on running. The mail order house would continue to ship to its customers. The steel company would continue to transport ore and process it into steel. The men grouped in these concerns would continue to do what they were accustomed to do. The community would still look to them for supply. Buyers from them would continue to pay their bills. Sellers to them would continue offering their wares. Plant executives would go down to the office as usual. The accounting offices would go on keeping the books under instructions from the comptroller. The laboratories would continue old experiments and plan new ones. In vain would some lawyer complain that the directors could no longer fix policy, or the president give orders. The directing group would still meet and make decisions. The president would still look to them to fix his pay, and his subordinates would look to the president for orders. Vacancies would be filled in the same manner as before, men found inadequate would be retired. The huge machine would keep right on rolling. This is of the essence of an institution, and not of a legalistic creation.

A remarkable illustration of this fact has been the attitude with which twentieth-century revolutionary governments dealt with great corporations. They have been encountered alike by Communist and Fascist states. Both by philosophy and by declared plan, Fascist and Communist states alike had not the slightest intention of leaving corporations (as Americans understood them) in existence. Communists proposed to make them coldly and simply branches of government. Fascists proposed to reduce them to more or less personal enclaves of power, tributary to a centralized and absolute dictatorship. Yet in all cases known to the writer, the approach of these governments to large corporations was conducted with extreme caution. Their first order was that the organizations should continue to function as usual. Their second was to substitute, gradually, officers who would follow orders from the central government or its relevant agencies. At inception, such orders were given with extreme care. In the Fascist case, especially, an attempt was made to hold the whole framework of the corporation together for a considerable period of time, the state retaining only the ultimate power of direction, choices of personnel, and, of course, the power of levying such tribute as the Fascist governors thought useful. The organizations were still intact after twenty years of Italian Fascist rule, and twelve years of Nazi administration. The Communist technique involved gradual infiltration, indoctrination of or control over the laboring staff as well, looking toward the day when the entire operation might be converted to statism. Though more rapid than the Fascist technique, the take-over process was a matter of years. In at least one of the satellite states of eastern

Europe in the year 1953 corporations were still functioning as entities which had been seized in 1945. Clearly the tenacity and strength of a well-organized corporate entity is thoroughly attested by experience, and heeded even by its bitterest enemies.

The businessman takes all this for granted. But the experienced student becomes excited. He knows that history is, among other things, the record of groupings of human beings which for some strange reason stay together: cities and states; churches and political parties; universities and clubs; nations and empires. The number of the units run into millions, but they can be classified in perhaps a dozen or so different types. This institution called the corporation is clearly one of a relatively small number of such types—and by no means the least important.

4

The foregoing justifies study of the modern corporation from the staging area of political science. But this involves somewhat wider responsibility than mere extension of our familiarity with this striking institution of the twentieth century. If our analysis is properly made, besides finding out more about corporations, we should learn something (a) about property and its relation to power; (b) about power, its habits, and perhaps its component elements; (c) about institutions which organize power in their relation to other organizations of power —for instance, the state. One result may be that we shall appreciate some of the problems necessarily forced upon the corporate institution in an individualistic, democratic society.

Perhaps it is as important to consider some of these questions as to consider the corporation itself. This is the stuff of pure political theory. It has been disregarded thus far, chiefly because in recent years pure theory in political science has received all too little attention. No apology is needed for dealing in pure theory. If explanations are in order, they had best be devoted to excusing the fact that more of this work has not been done earlier.

Out of the theory it will appear that the modern corporation as an institution is entitled to much more respect than it has frequently received. The dangers inherent in its use are also great enough to require serious attention. The possibilities of its continued development are, so far as one can see, unlimited. It is, in fact, an institution at a cross road in history, capable of becoming one of the master tools of society—capable also of surprising abuse; worthy of the attention of the community as well as of scholars.

5

The main outlines of the twentieth-century revolution are only now beginning to be dimly discernible. The drama of the Russian revolution from 1917 to the present, and associated Communist revolutions in neighboring countries, so occupied the foreground that the entire movement went comparatively unnoticed. The fact appears to be that from and after World War I the entire world was in revolution, and the base of that revolution was technical far more than it was social. Changes in human life and habits, modification of human institutions, and expansion of human horizons occurred everywhere. The philosophical and scientific discoveries of the nineteenth century were put to work in the twentieth, and whole civilizations changed as a result. The Russian revolution was nominally based on Communist dogma; but its significant struggle was to find some instrument by which a vast backward country could be mauled into industrialization. The capitalist revolution in which the United States was the leader found apter, more efficient and more flexible means through collectivizing capital in corporations. When the whole story is told it will, I believe, be found that the chief impetus to the Communist state as an instrument was the insistence in backward countries that they plunge toward the results of an industrial revolution which was leaving them behind. This, of course, is the precise opposite of the Marxian dogma. Elsewhere the Marxist state seemed a brutal, blunt, and fumbling instrument; capitalism was evolving its own instruments, and accomplishing the twentieth-century revolution with infinitely more humanity and efficiency. The fundamental change was technical: the application to the everyday life of hundreds of millions of people of newly developed methods of production. Economics necessarily developed with that change; politics was modified by the economics; the social theory has yet to be written. The Russian, the German and Italian Fascist, the British Socialist, the American capitalist revolutions all were, and still are, driven by this underlying force. None of them have completed their course.

In this aspect, it is justifiable to consider the American corporation not as a business device but as a social institution in the context of a revolutionary century.

II

Corporate Power and Modern Capitalism

The two most notable achievements of the twentieth-century corporations have been their ability to concentrate economic power in themselves and their ability to increase production and distribution. Apparently the power is essential to the productivity (Professor J. K. Galbraith of Harvard seems to think so), though that relationship is not definitively established. Actually they do go together, which is all we need to know for the moment.

The extent of the concentration of power may be very briefly stated, since our real interest is in the politics rather than the economics of the situation. According to a most careful and wholly unbiased estimate —that of Professor M. A. Adelman of Massachusetts Institute of Technology—135 corporations own 45 per cent of the industrial assets of the United States—or nearly one-fourth of the manufacturing volume of the entire world. This represents a concentration of economic ownership greater perhaps than any yet recorded in history. Adelman's computation suggests that this is a static condition varying slightly from year to year but increasing or decreasing, if at all, "at the pace of a glacial drift." Accepting this, it is still a sufficiently impressive fact on the American economic landscape.

We cannot, however, leave the quantitative estimate quite there. Large corporations, in and of themselves, are impressive vehicles of power. Not less interesting is the fact that in a considerable and growing number of industries (covering at a rough estimate 70 per cent of all American industry) a pattern has emerged—that which we may christen the "concentrate." American law, if not American economics, has in general prevented monopoly. But it has sanctioned and perhaps even encouraged a system, industry by industry, in which a few large corporations dominate the trade. Two or three, or at most, five, corporations will have more than half the business, the remainder being divided among a greater or less number of smaller concerns who must necessarily live within the conditions made for them by the "Big Two" or "Big Three" or "Big Five" as the case may be. Adequate studies, including two by the Twentieth Century Fund (*How Big Is Big Business?*, 1937, and *Monopoly and Free Enterprise*, Drs. G. W. Stocking and M. W. Watkins, 1951) perhaps give the best picture of the changed structure of American economy. A somewhat older study, by Dr. Clair Wilcox, *Competition and Monopoly in American Industry,* forms one of the monographs in the report of the Temporary National Economic Committee. Statisticians will struggle with the figures. There will be little dispute, however, with the main conclusion: considerably more than half of all American industry—and that the most important half—is operated by "concentrates." Slightly more than half is owned outright by not more than 200 corporations. This is calculated on the coldest basis—the amount of actual assets owned by the corporations involved.

We are not excused, however, from looking beyond the simple arithmetic of property actually owned by corporations. The impact of many corporations—for example, General Motors or the great oil companies—goes beyond the confines of their actual ownership. For example, at a rough estimate, some three billions of dollars are invested in garages and facilities owned by so-called "small" businessmen who hold agency contracts from the principal automobile manufacturers. The owners are small, independent businessmen usually trading as "corporations" but certainly not giants. They are, nominally, independent. But their policies, operations, and, in large measure, their prices, are determined by the motor company whose cars they sell. The same is true of the "small businessman" who "owns" a gasoline-filling station. The ability of the large corporation to make decisions and direct operations overflows the area of its ownership. Its power travels farther than its title—in fact, a great deal farther, even though a statistical estimate of the extent of this peripheral belt is still lacking. There are other, less spectacular, methods by which the power of the central organism is extended beyond the nominal borders of its ownership—patent licenses, for example.

In any case, the aggregate result is hardly open to dispute. The mid-twentieth-century American capitalist system depends on and revolves around the operations of a relatively few very large corporations. It pivots upon industries most of which are concentrated in the hands of extremely few corporate units. Materially, the community has profited mightily. The system of large-scale production and mass distribution carried on by means of these large institutions can fairly claim the greatest share of credit. The face of the country has been changed. Poverty, in the sense that it is understood elsewhere in the world, in America is reduced to minimal proportions. Professor Louis Hacker of Columbia not unjustifiably calls it the "triumph of American capitalism."

It is our task to dig a little below the surface, to try to understand what this system is, and whither it may be bound. Perhaps excavation may be prefaced with a brief excursion into pure theory.

2

Property, theoretically considered, has two sets of attributes. On the one hand it can be a medium for creation and production and development. On the other, it offers possibility for reception, enjoyment, and consumption. An old-fashioned farm or small business property held by a single owner or small group of owners combined both groups of attributes in the same hands. The owner used his property to create, to produce, to improve. In a word, he used it as capital. He also used it to provide for his needs and for his enjoyment—in other words, for his consumption. Life was all in one piece, and the attributes were intertwined.

This did something to and for an owner as well as to and for the property. It gave him a task to do and an outlet for his creative ability, small or great. It gave him a livelihood, and possibly more. The attributes of creation and the attributes of reception were not separated, or at any rate were complemented one by the other and the man was the result. Jefferson's picture of the ideal United States was a country in which none was very rich; none very poor: all were producers, all owners and consumers. The Homestead Acts permitting settlement of the public lands were precisely aimed to stimulate this individual and possessory ownership of property.

The twentieth-century corporation has proved to be the great instrumentality by which these two groups of property attributes have been separated one from the other. The process was inevitable, granting that modern organizations of production and distribution must be so large as to be incapable of being owned by any individual or small group of individuals. It was foreshadowed, perhaps, when the first promoters conceived the plan of distributing stock in an enterprise to be run by a Board of Managers—a device practiced in England at least as early as the sixteenth century. Only in the twentieth century has the process been conducted to an extent which revolutionizes national life.

In effect, when an individual invests capital in the large corporation, he grants to the corporate management all power to use that capital to create, produce, and develop, and he abandons all control over the product. He keeps a modified right to receive a portion of the profits, usually in the form of money, and a highly enhanced right to sell his participation for cash. He is an almost completely inactive recipient. He can spend his dividends or sell his shares for cash, taking care of his needs for consumption or enjoyment. But he must look elsewhere for opportunity to produce or create. Were the American system entirely one of ownership and production by large corporations, every individual would have a job under the direction of corporate managers, and in addition to his salary, he would have whatever dividends he might receive from investments; but in any case the two functions would be entirely split. There is a striking analogy between this and socialist theory. Under socialism, all productive property is held or "owned" by the agencies of the socialist state; all individuals receive pay or benefits. Planning, development, creation, production, and so forth is done by the political agency; the individual, presumably, receives his share of the product.

Within the corporation, the management disposes of the aggregate possibility of use, production, and creation in respect of the assets it has collected. Nominally, the corporate management receives this by authority of its stockholders; factually, the process is not a matter of choice on either side. 1,100,000 shareholders could not possibly run American Telephone & Telegraph Company; indeed it is highly improbable that that number of individuals could run anything. No large enterprise could possibly go forward except under a unified and concentrated system of organization and command. If modern civilization and technical development require enterprises of size to provide the standard of living the American community expects, they require precisely this split of property into its component attributes, assigning the receptive attributes to the group of shareholders, and gathering the creative attributes in a single command.

Concentration of these creative functions in the hands of a small group produces the phenomenon we call "power." Quite simply, this is capacity to induce or require action by others in certain areas of activity.

We know little about power. As a phenomenon in political science, so far as the writer knows, it has never been well analyzed theoretically, nor even well described. We know that it is inseparably bound to institutional organization, of which also we know very little. As it relates to large corporations, certain aspects may be noted, though the list cannot be exhaustive.

A corporation management has power to direct the activities of its subordinate officers and employees. Peripherally, this includes power to give or deny employment and to affect wage standards of its competitors. Sometimes when there is countervailing concentration of power in other institutions—for example, great labor unions—the decision of a large corporation in respect of wage scale and labor negotiation can and frequently does settle the wage scales and standards for the entire industry.

The management has power to determine whether and how it will carry on operations. This may include power to determine that certain towns or areas shall be developed and shall become industrialized, and heretofore has included (the power is now in dispute) capacity to leave a community, taking its operations elsewhere, possibly leaving a broken city behind.

The corporate management can determine what markets it will supply—no American law yet exists requiring any corporation to go into or develop a market it does not choose to serve. In some industries—for example, electric light and power—this can be the power to accelerate regional development in one area, and refuse it to another. Likewise corporate managers can, within limits, determine what kind of goods and services they will produce and sell. This last is severely limited: they must either meet a public desire or create it, and creation of public desire is difficult and expensive. The success of the American tobacco companies in making the United States a nation of cigarette smokers sufficiently indicates that under some circumstances it can be done.

Corporate managers have power to forward and pursue technical development within the general scope of their enterprises, and to determine the speed with which they will push that development. The singular productivity of the American corporate system has perhaps proceeded from the fact that most American corporations made comparatively full use of that power.

Within limits, the corporate managers may enter into the process of forming public opinion, and some of them do this though the extent of the exercise of that power is a matter of dispute.

Finally, it lies within the power of corporate managers to decide (within limits) the extent and rate of capital expansion. While no one corporation alone can affect events very much, this power aggregated in, say, the 200 largest corporations, may make the difference whether the national economy advances or retards. Early in 1954 the General Motors management decided to commit more than a billion dollars in new capital development and at least one of the motives was said to have been their feeling that this would tend to balance retrograde tendencies which might lead to depression.

All of these powers, though to an infinitesimal degree, inhered in individuals under the system of individualized, possessory property prevailing one hundred and fifty years ago. The difference lies in the fact that no one individual could seriously affect or direct the actions of other individuals: he could only decide for himself. Results in an economic system of that kind were thus attained without conscious intent or decision by anyone; they were the product of an unplanned aggregate. Mid-twentieth-century capitalism has been given the power and the means of more or less planned economy, in which decisions are or at least can be taken in the light of their probable effect on the whole community.

3

The argument is promptly made, both by scholars and by businessmen, that this power we have been discussing, if it exists at all, is not absolute, and that it is severely limited. There is force in the contention, but on examination the contention has less force than its proponents frequently assert. Some of the checks and balances alleged to exist upon this power require re-examination in the light of facts.

It is said that the power of corporate management is severely limited by the standards and public opinion prevailing in the capital market; that a management must in using these powers conform to the norms of behavior expected of them by investors whose capital they may seek. This was one of the tenets of the classical economists. In theory, the corporate entrepreneur from time to time had to go into the capital markets seeking funds: to add this plant, to increase the size of his existing business; or possibly to establish a new business. In practice this meant that he had to submit the enterprise operation to the scrutiny and judgment of investors or to the investment banking houses who represented investors. This was a formidable limitation on his power: so formidable indeed that members or representatives of investment banking houses commonly requested a foothold in the councils of the enterprise. Familiarly this was done by placing one or more directors on the corporation's board. In addition, account had to be taken of that current of public opinion which prevails in the financial world and which powerfully affects the views of individuals who have money to invest. This segment of public opinion was, and still is, relatively narrow. It moves along lines which frequently differ from broad public opinion swings of the kind evidenced in national or even local elections. Nevertheless in its own fashion, it acted as a sort of informal referendum. Economists refer to it as "the judgment of the market place." In economic theory this "judgment of the market place" is assumed to be a powerful controlling factor. By declining to provide capital, it could, in theory, check overexpansion; could favor enterprises which the country needed most (and to which it was, therefore, presumably prepared to pay larger returns through higher prices and profits); it could penalize or perhaps displace inefficient management, and so forth.

There was a time, unquestionably, when the "judgment of the market place," executed by willingness or unwillingness to invest, was a significant factor. Its extent is not certain: the writer knows of no statistical computations. The assumption was made by Adam Smith in 1776 in the *Wealth of Nations,* and has been steadily carried forward. The point of importance is that the assumption has lost most of its validity in mid-twentieth century.

In November 1953, the economists for the National City Bank made an excellent brief study of the use and sources of capital. Their conclusions confirmed earlier computations made by the writer and Dr. Irvin S. Bussing, then economist for the Savings Banks Trust Company in New York. They calculated that in eight years (1946 to 1953 inclusive) an aggregate of 150 billions of dollars had been spent in the United States for capital expenditures, namely, modernizing and enlarging plant and equipment. This was spent by all of American business (excluding, of course, financial corporations like banks and insurance companies which deal not in physical assets but in money, credit, or evi-

37

dence of debt of one kind or another). The figure is not surprising: the increase in American industrial plant was enormous and huge amounts of capital were needed. The spectacular fact is the source of this huge amount.

Sixty-four per cent of the 150 billion came from "internal sources," that is to say, receipts of the enterprises which had been accumulated and not distributed as dividends. Included in this figure (about 99 billion) were (1) retained earnings and (2) reserves set aside for depreciation, depletion, and amortization on past debt. Retained earnings were, of course, far and away the largest proportion.

Of the remaining 51 billion, or 36 per cent of the total, one-half was raised by current borrowing, chiefly represented (directly or indirectly) by bank credit. This accounts for approximately 25½ billion.

Eighteen billion, or 12 per cent of the total, was raised by issue of bonds or notes. This may fairly be said to have run the gauntlet of "market-place judgment," though the impact of it was changed and perhaps somewhat restricted by the fact that probably half of this amount was "privately placed." A private placement means that the enterprise does not offer bonds or securities for general subscription or purchase to the public; it negotiates with a large institution such as an insurance company or perhaps a syndicate of several such companies which buy all the issue.

Six per cent, or 9 billion, out of the total of 150 billion was raised by issue of stock. Here, and here only, do we begin to approach the "risk capital" investment so much relied on by classic economic theory. Even here a considerable amount was as far removed from "risk" as the situation permitted: without exact figures, apparently a majority of the 9 billion was represented by preferred stock. Probably not more than 5 billion of the total amount was represented by common stock —the one situation in which an investor considers an enterprise, decides on its probable usefulness and profitability, and puts down his savings, aware of a degree of risk but hoping for large profit.

There is substantial evidence, which need not be reviewed here, that this is representative of the real pattern of the twentieth-century capitalism. The capital is there; and so is capitalism. The waning factor is the capitalist. He has somehow vanished in great measure from the picture, and with him has vanished much of the controlling force of his market-place judgment. He is not extinct: roughly a billion dollars a year (say 5 per cent of total savings) is invested by him; but he is no longer a decisive force. In his place stand the boards of directors of corporations, chiefly large ones, who retain profits and risk them in expansion of the business along lines indicated by the circumstances of their particular operation. Not the public opinion of the market place with all the economic world from which to choose, but the directoral opinion of corporate managers as to the line of greatest opportunity within their own concern, now chiefly determines the application of risk capital. Major corporations in most instances do not seek capital. They form it themselves.

There are, undoubtedly, powerful exceptions to this trend. Utility companies, both in old industries such as telephone and electric light and power, and in new, such as those in the natural gas business, still seek and get large amounts of capital through the market place. But the number of enterprises, and the amount of capital they seek, has proportionably diminished. For practical purposes, the judgment of the market place in relation to application of capital has little application in the greatest and most dynamic areas of American industry.

Let us put this development into the context of our central problem of corporate power. The brief review above given even without other evidence which is available fairly justifies the conclusion that one of the classic checks on corporate power has been weakened, where it has not been removed altogether. A corporation like

General Electric or General Motors which steadily builds its own capital, does not need to submit itself and its operations to the judgment of the financial markets. Power assumed to be brought under the review of banking and investment opinion a generation ago is now reviewed and checked chiefly by the conscience of its directors and managers.

Lest this be considered criticism, let it be said at once that removal of the market place as ultimate arbiter of capital application has probably enhanced and certainly has not diminished the rate of American industrial progress. Market-place judgment was rendered chiefly by investment bankers; and there is a difference of opinion whether it helped or hurt. Willingness of individuals, and bankers and institutions representing them, to invest money, is based primarily on a favorable forecast of the probable future of the enterprise. But since the future is still mercifully concealed from the knowledge of men and investors, the usual criterion for judgment is the record of past experience. This perhaps is why judgment of the market place usually tends to be "conservative." As a rule it does not readily or cheaply provide risk capital for new and untried revolutionary inventions, or for expansion of enterprise into the unexplored regions of science (though there are conspicuous exceptions). But a board of directors of the quality maintained by, let us say, General Electric, of necessity must be familiar with the product of laboratories and research and fully appreciative of the "long-haired know-how," to quote a bit of plant slang. It has had experience in translating novel ideas and applications of abstract science into a product or service capable of being sold at a profit. Pioneering which would be a mystery to an individual investor and difficult to appraise even for an investment banker, is part of the day's work in many of the greater modern corporations. Indeed, if the corporation be large enough, the risk inevitably incurred in pioneering a new field can be "averaged"—ten pioneering operations may be carried on at the same time; losses incurred in operations which fail can be more than made up by profits reaped from those which succeed. A large corporation not only can form and dispose of "risk capital"; it has the experience, and the will, the organization, and the business position enabling it to take the risk and follow through to a conclusion. If release from market-place judgment increases corporate power on the presently available evidence, it cannot be said that in terms of material development the community has suffered.

4

Other students of the corporate system, among them some of the ablest commentators, consider that though power has indeed been concentrated through the corporate system, it is quite adequately held in check by the existence of competition. Recently, Professor Sumner Schlichter of Harvard in a brilliant essay published by the *Atlantic Monthly* asserted accurately that even within a concentrate competition exists, often of the bitterest kind. Monopoly in general has been avoided. Also there is competition between products. This is true. Not only does General Electric compete with Westinghouse, and Ford with General Motors, but goods and services offered by any one industry are checked by the possibility that other industries will offer substitute goods or services. Unreasonable exaction by railroads will force goods onto trucks. Overpricing coal will merely lead to increased use of oil. Conceivably (though happily it has not happened yet) oppressive charges by motor companies might lead everyone to learn to fly helicopters. There is solid force in these contentions. Certainly in primary commodities even a king in its own field like steel must keep a weather eye out for the possibility that aluminum may be used instead, while aluminum must always watch out for magnesium. Therefore, argue these scholars, concentration of economic power is bounded vertically by competition within industry and horizontally by competition from other products or services capable of being substituted for them.

The fact may be immediately admitted. Admitted, *arguendo,* that a concentration of power proportionately has remained more or less static—though the writer would make that admission only tentatively—there is considerable evidence the other way. Elsewhere it has been noted that the power of General Motors is not limited by its assets, but extends to its dealer relationships as well; and the same phenomenon appears in a large number of other peripheral relationships. These have never been measured. Also, the statistical estimates given by Professor Adelman relate only to operating manufacturing companies, and do not touch what are called "financial corporations"—the great insurance companies, the great banks, and the newer but rapidly growing pension funds. These buy securities in corporations; thus far they have ordinarily leaned over backward in not entering the management of the companies whose securities they buy. But it does not follow at all that as their assets continue to grow (they do) and their holdings of securities of operating corporations continue to increase (as they inevitably must) that they can indefinitely remain spectators of the corporations whose stock and bonds furnish the vehicle for their investments. If they wished they could even today exercise a powerful choice in managements of many of the corporations measured by Adelman; and their ability to do this seems likely to increase. Not often in history does the holder of potential power decline to use it. Data on concentration of power (as contrasted with data on concentration of asset-ownership) is far from complete.

But having made the admissions, it is submitted that the conclusions drawn by Professor Schlichter and his colleagues scarcely follow. At the very least it can be said that competition within the system of corporate concentrates produces results quite different from the balanced economy expounded by Adam Smith. The reason for this lies in the fact that competition means one thing when thousands of tradesmen, craftsmen, or farmers are offering their wares to thousands of customers. It means quite another when four or five large units are grinding against each other. The result of the competitive system when many units were involved was to push out the least efficient units, or perhaps the worst-placed strategically. The result of great corporations fighting each other is either consolidation, or elimination of one of the units, or acceptance of a situation in which the place of each is approximately respected.

The first effect of competition within a concentrate is to eliminate many, perhaps most, of the so-called "independents"—the crowd of smaller unit competitors. They may be eliminated by bankruptcy, or they may be consolidated into a single organization capable of maintaining itself. In either case many small units disappear. Carried to extremes—as was the case in the last half of the nineteenth century—the result was monopoly. Today even the relatively frail legislative barrier of the antitrust laws have inhibited that: no one wishes to risk the possibility of dissolution even though the last substantial dissolution by court decree took place a generation ago when the Standard Oil Company was broken up in 1921. Perhaps one should include termination of a monopoly that was not imposed by judicial decree but rather through a combination of law, industry, and government—the erection of the three-company aluminum concentrate in 1948 which left the properties of Aluminum Company of America substantially intact, but erected two large-scale corporate competitors alongside of it. The ultimate in concentration—concentration of all companies in the single monopolistic concern—has been generally prevented. The concentrate has been accepted. This very fact, however, emphasizes that the end of competition where large-scale units are involved is quite different from that where a vast number of small units is concerned. Analyzed, competition within a concentrate is more a struggle for power to balance supply against demand than to secure customers by price competition. Indeed in a recent essay in the *Harvard Business Review,* Professor J. Kenneth Galbraith, after pointing out that price competition plays a minor role, insists that when business is defending itself "a claim of intense and virtuous competition is something to be avoided like the plague"—and in any event the claim is unnecessary.

Again, competition within a concentrate (and to some extent competition within a vast number of producers in the twentieth century) has commonly produced a political rather than an economic effect. The oil industry by an N.R.A. Code in 1933, and later by the interstate oil compact and its accompanying legislation, forthrightly adjusted supply to demand by the forthright process of administrative limitation. Every month the Bureau of Mines estimates probable demand and state regulative commissions tell oil producers in their respective states how much crude oil they can bring out of their wells. The scheme is intended to assure that the oil, brought above ground, shall (when imports are added) correspond substantially to the

American demand. The plan has worked successfully for two decades. The American sugar industry follows somewhat the same plan, though the mechanics are different; since suppliers of raw sugar are chiefly outside the United States, the adjustment of supply to demand is accomplished by the Secretary of Agriculture who has been given power to fix the quota of raw sugar which may be imported. He fixes it against estimates of probable demand for sugar products.

Other and different schemes, in varying states of development, prevail in other industries. The point is that competition where concentrates are concerned is rarely if ever permitted to carry through to its logical result. Nobody, it seems, wants that.

As a result, competition in mid-twentieth century leads more often to a political than to an economic resolution of events. Supply is not equated to demand by bankrupting or eliminating suppliers save perhaps at the end of a very long sequence of events generally noncommercial in value. Equation is reached by an industrial plan controlling the industry.

In some industries like transportation and public utilities, solution by competition was discarded from the very outset, and state regulation adopted in its place. Today, the system of more or less planned industry has spread far beyond the enterprise classically assumed to be "natural monopoly." An incomplete list of the areas of American economy presently controlled would include: banks, and banking—via the Federal Reserve legislation; railroads and trucks—via the Interstate Commerce Act and companion legislation; electric light and power—via the Federal Power Commission Act; and certain sections of the Securities and Exchange Commission legislation; radio and television—via the Federal Communications Act; oil and petroleum—via the Interstate Oil Compact of 1925 and the Connally Hot Oil Act; shipping and merchant marine—through the Maritime Commission legislation; meat products— through the Packers and Stockyards legislation. In lesser degree of development the aluminum industry is at the moment operating under a jerry-rigged plan combined out of an antitrust decree against Alcoa and federal administrative action constructing the Reynolds Metal Company and Kaiser Aluminum Company; the sugar refining industry under the Sugar Act of 1948; the aviation transport industry under the Civil Aeronautics Act, and aviation production chiefly by administrative action through the purchasing agencies of the Department of Defense. Lesser, but effective private arrangements, often achieved by mere balance of power in a concentrate, and without agreement-violating antitrust laws, are often more numerous.

49

A tendency to seek agreed solutions rather than abide the result of competition has been widely deplored in many quarters. Professor Hayek at the University of Chicago especially considers this trend a plain step on the road to serfdom, and does not weary in his attempt to persuade the country to abandon its propensity for these primrose paths to perdition. Obstinately, however, big business and small business, farmers and laborers, corporations which like their profit margins and labor unions which like their jobs, controlling majorities in the Republican as well as the Democratic parties, decline to acknowledge the error of their ways. They refuse to march to the mourners' bench, and resist the doctrine that economic forces left to themselves will produce a desirable result. The oil industry could hardly be accused of creeping Socialism; but it wanted the N.R.A. Code and later the interstate oil compact and its regulatory machinery. The writer's associates in the sugar industry are rarely accused of Marxian sympathies; but they insisted on and got the Sugar Act of 1948. Mr. Herbert Hoover is not commonly ranked as a collectivist; but it was his administration which started the farm program later developed under Mr. Henry Wallace and, on the whole, maintained thus far by a Republican Congress under President Eisenhower. The rude fact appears to be that when 45 per cent of

American industry is dominated by 135 corporations which necessarily must administer their prices, no one else is going to risk the logical results of wholly free competition. In blunt fact, competition in an industry dominated by two or three large units is not the same as competition between thousands of small units. In a school of herring each herring may compete with the other for the available food supply. But herring do not compete with whales. And competition of whales between themselves is more like war than economics. It is known by economists as "imperfect competition" Mr. Arthur R. Burns, now Professor of Economics at Columbia University, writing a book describing it in 1938, called it *The Decline of Competition*. The result of competition within a concentrated industry is some sort of price stabilization. At the very least it is clear that competition operates within far narrower limits than classical economics contemplated; realistically, it is only a partial check.

The reason is clear enough, at least to political scientists. Few of the major segments in a community really want a regime of unlimited competition in the modern community—neither the great corporations, nor their labor, nor their suppliers. Fundamentally, they all want, not a perpetual struggle, but a steady job—the job of producing goods at a roughly predictable cost under roughly predictable conditions, so that goods can be sold in the market at a roughly predictable price.

Their reasoning has a solid basis behind it. Competition between thousands of people from time to time eliminating marginal groups of inefficient producers likewise produces only marginal hardship. A struggle between giants may wreck hundreds of thousands of lives and whole communities. In a system of individual entrepreneurs the men squeezed out of one market may readily turn to another; in the highly organized concentrate, change-over is always difficult and expensive, and often impossible.

In a system of corporate concentration the result of competition is some sort of planning; and planning does not reduce power but increases it.

5

If, as it seems, the two chief economic checks on corporate power no longer have their old vitality, are other checks emerging?

The question cannot be answered yet. Indeed, finding the right answer is likely to be one of the great problems of American political organization in the second half of the twentieth century. It must be set against the European context. There, Communist doctrine set up the managers of corporations as part of a class to be destroyed while the organizations themselves must be integrated into a state machine. Fascist and National Socialist doctrine looked toward seizing and holding corporate institutions intact, and using them as agencies for political and economic domination of a disfranchized people. Democracy has, perhaps fortunately, developed no theory. Instead it has rather naively assumed, without evidence, that great corporations would remain as part of an economic complex in balance. Only the lone voice of J. Kenneth Galbraith has been raised to suggest that American capitalism will turn on the balance of institutional forces—he, quite rightly, calls his study, *American Capitalism: the Concept of Countervailing Power,* and assumes that the principal power institutions will be, respectively, the great corporations operating industrial oligopoly on one hand and the great industrial labor unions on the other. Professor Kenneth E. Boulding of the University of Michigan in 1953 discussed the problem in somewhat the same vein, describing the American system as the product of the *Organizational Revolution;* he accepts intervention of the state to a considerable degree as politically inevitable, but expresses the hope that ethical considerations will dominate the contending institutions and hold the resulting complex in balance. Clearly, if business organizations like the modern corporation are not automatically limited by economics, a political problem of first importance is in the making.

Limitation does exist, in the belief of this writer. Though the lines are obscure and the evidence meager, the factual material suggests two major forces tending to keep the modern American corporation a serviceable rather than a tyrannous institution.

The first is, quite clearly, the force of public opinion, which may translate itself into political action in a great variety of ways—and which therefore is heeded before it has so translated itself.

Diverse illustrations may be given. Thus, just prior to World War II the head of one of the great oil companies was thought to have laid down a policy authorizing sale of petroleum through a neutral country to Nazi Germany, contrary to the general policy of the United States and to the overwhelming body of public opinion. A public clamor resulted and the corporation relieved the officer of his post. Again immediately after the close of the war, the American market was hungry for automobiles; a new car could command almost any price the producer cared to ask. The major automobile companies declined to take full advantage of this situation, holding their list prices far below the prices obviously obtainable and actually prevailing in the black market, and did something at least to prevent their less socially minded dealer organizations from overcharging. A somewhat similar price policy—contrary, be it noted, to the dictates of supply and demand —was followed in 1947 by the larger steel companies, and in certain of its lines, by General Electric. Less far-seeing corporate organizations have occasionally rebuffed public opinion. In 1932 the rural regions of the United States had only slight access to electric power, and there was great agitation for extension of power lines to farming and sparsely settled areas. The light and power companies considered or, at all events, stated, that they could not do this. The United States government thereupon authorized rural electrification, first as a relief project, but eventually crystallizing the operation in the Rural Electrification Authority. This body only had authority to finance; but, stimulated by Mr. Murray Lincoln of the Farm Bureau Co-operative Association, it called into existence farmers' co-operatives in all regions and made available to them financing, engineering service and planning, and technical information. Rural electrification began to spring up in many parts of the country, whereupon the light and power companies discovered unsuspected ability to serve this market, and proceeded to do it. In the ensuing fifteen years, the number of American farms to which electric power was made available jumped from

30 per cent to 90 per cent, of which more than half obtained service from private enterprise under the spur of possible government-financed competition. Still another instance: after the war it became clear that demand for steel in the United States had been underestimated by the industry; political agitation resulted, and in his 1949 inaugural address, President Truman suggested the possibility that the United States government might itself undertake operation of additional facilities for steel production. The steel companies did not abide the event; they increased American steel-producing capacity by more than 20 per cent in the ensuing five years. Without adding illustrations, it is sufficient to say that a modern American corporation understands well enough that it has a "constituency" to deal with. If its constituents—notably its buyers—are unsatisfied, they will go to the political state for solution. Hardly any present-day board of directors or corporation management would take the position that it could afford to disregard public opinion—or would last very long if it did.

This, it appears, is the chief balance, and it is frankly a political one. Its advantage is its pragmatic quality. American public opinion is directly practical and not, as a rule, doctrinaire. It did not want "public ownership" of rural electrification lines; it did want readily available electricity at low rates. There is no passionate desire to have the instruments of production in the hands of the state: there is a vivid and very active desire to have the production needed by the community available on terms which the community recognizes as substantially fair. There has been considerable public suspicion of concentration of power in great corporations; but then there has also been considerable public apprehension of undue centralized power in the government —or, for that matter, of undue concentration of power anywhere. Thus far, the force of public opinion has been able to balance any centralized power wherever it has appeared and appeared to be oppressive.

A disadvantage (not peculiar perhaps to a political as contrasted with an economic balancing force) is the fact that movements of public opinion tend to be sluggish in commencing, and extreme once they start. A situation has to be really out of hand before public pressure begins to assert itself, and when it does passions run high. Many, perhaps most, of the proceedings brought by the Department of Justice under the antitrust laws, or initiated by the Federal Trade Commission, stem directly from nascent public opinion movements. Exact justice cannot be expected in these situations: someone gets hurt. Yet on the whole community standards for corporate action gradually do assert themselves, and capable corporations reach for them and endeavor to meet them.

A second check is implicit in the system of oligopoly as contrasted with either monopoly or socialism; it is the real reason why oligopoly, however imperfect, is always preferable to monopoly. When there is more than one unit in the business, one of them will inevitably strive for the leadership position. Each may and commonly does tacitly limit its competition with its giant colleagues, but will rarely carry the limitation to extremes. If any one of the giants in the field can find a way to take advantage of a colleague's mistakes, of its omission to keep up with technical advance, of its failure to meet the minimal standards laid down by public opinion, the opportunity will be seized. The most typical concentrated industry in the United States which thus far has not become subject to a politically adopted plan is the motors industry. The endless maneuvering for leadership position between Ford and General Motors is an almost classic instance of competition within oligopoly. Somewhat the same situation prevails in the electronics field where General Electric and Westinghouse are continuously in tacit agreement —and continuously at war.

Behind and beyond these two major checks there is always the political power of the state. Only in times of great travail is it seriously invoked. But it is there; and few men who have watched private industry become statist in half the world overseas underrate its possibilities. If there is no dogma of statism in the United States, neither would preference for private enterprise defend private enterprise very long if it ceased to satisfy community standards. The real guarantee of nonstatist industrial organization in America is a substantially satisfied public.

This poses perhaps the unsolved problem of the next generation. It has been said, perhaps with truth, that much of the chaos in much of the old world arises from the demands of the masses for a standard of living beyond the capacity of their productive enterprises. Not getting it, resort is had to governments, which have been less successful in augmenting production in these areas than private industry here. So far at least th sectors of the American public whose opinion makes demands on industry—labor, consumers, and to a lesser degree, suppliers of material—have limited their demands to the possible—a much higher "possible" it is true in the United States than exists anywhere else on earth. A clear and fair statement by corporation managements of what they can and cannot do is commonly received with a surprising degree of consideration by the corporate constituency.

This perhaps underlines the most powerful single imperative imposed on corporate management: it must tell the truth, and so conduct itself that it retains the confidence of its customers, its labor, its suppliers and the sector of the public with whom it deals. In the corporate situation this is the equivalent of the "just consent of the governed." The corporation is now, essentially, a nonstatist political institution, and its directors are in the same boat with public office-holders. If ever corporate managers base their continued tenure on power and not on reason, the end is disaster.

III

The Conscience of the King and of the Corporation

William, Conqueror-King of England and Duke of Normandy, had died at Rouen. At a beautiful church at St. Etienne de Caen, a throng of nobles, bishops, soldiers, clerks, and common people assembled to pay their last respects. The funeral offices had been said, and the pallbearers were about to lower the old Duke's body into the tomb prepared for it.

Then an obscure man, Asselin by name, broke from the crowd, with the one clamor which could stop so great a ceremony. He cried, "Haro!"

The proceedings stopped then and there. It was Asselin's right to state his grievance. It was simple: this land, this ground on which the church rose in stately columns, belonged to his father and him. Duke William had taken it by force, and made no reparation. The very grave was on the site of his family homestead. The bishops consulted and promptly made arrangements. They paid at once sixty sous in token compensation for the few square feet of earth in which the Duke was now to be buried. They promised compensation for the land taken. Then, and only then, was William the Conqueror interred; and there the beautiful Abbey still stood when the American armies, storming in from Omaha Beach in World War II, recaptured Caen from a foreign foe. So the story comes down through the account of Augustin Thierry, and it bears every mark of being substantially true.

The "Haro" cry had long been known in Norman law. It was the recognized means of appeal to the conscience of feudal power. It is said—no one really knows —that William's predecessor, the Northman, Duke Rollo, had had statesmanship enough to see that justice must go with power and he had gone in person from place to place in Normandy, directing that all who suffered wrong at the hands of his neighbor, or of the feudal officers, or even from the Duke himself, should cry, "Ha! Rollo!" whereupon the Duke must listen to his cause, deciding it according to the law of God and good conscience. In any event, it had become a fixed Norman custom. In somewhat different form a like appeal was the practice in England from and after the Conquest. As we shall note in a moment, it is probably one of the origins of the British law of equity. Even in Normandy, tossed by recurrent feudal storms, it became the basis of a special jurisdiction (there presently emerged Norman judges of "Haro," competent to give extraordinary relief remarkably similar to the relief dispensed by British Chancellors and equity courts). Undisputedly the sovereign and his lords had power. But besides power, there were also conceptions of right, and morality, and justice. From these even the king was not exempt. In the western world at least the phenomenon is familiar wherever more or less absolute power appears.

2

It seems a far cry from Norman dukes to corporation managements. But it is suggested that the phenomenon of power is enduring, and the distance not so great.

The power we have been considering, though limited, is in large measure absolute. Around its use the law authorizes a mantle of sanctity, the legal "presumption" that management action is taken for the best interests of the corporate institution. Behind this presumption lies great persuasion of fact. No outside court, no legislature, no group of laymen, even relatively few business peers are competent to pass on whether a given decision was wise or foolish, sound or hazardous, technically justified or hopelessly unfounded. Only where wisdom is carried to the extremity of obvious folly, hazard is indulged to the point of recklessness, technical considerations are disregarded to the point of irrationality, or the decision tainted by corruption, can outsiders pass judgment. Hindsight obviously proves something; the event of any decision indicates whether it is well taken; the aggregate of all decisions add up to a total of success or failure. But the standard of decision-taking has to be in the light of a situation as it stands when the course is charted and the die cast. Within a wide range, management power is absolute.

It could hardly be otherwise. If every decision by management were reviewable on all of its merits, the reviewing authority—court, investigating commission, regulatory authority, or whatnot—would be, in the old phrase "substituting its business judgment for the business judgment of management." In effect it would be running the business. If anything is settled it is that the exercise of power within the range of its permissible use is lonely business. Within that range the true judge is the conscience of the man or men who act.

The fact, and the legal recognition of it, offer a striking parallel to the classic political doctrine that the king could do no wrong. As in the case of the corporation, this was partly recognition of the fact that the authority of the state was essential to peace and partly acceptance of the fact that none save the wielder of authority would ever know enough of the whole situation, its implications and its perils, to pass judgment on the merits. If authority to act is ever resigned or referred to others, the institution breaks down. In Shakespeare's play, *King Lear,* the king courts disaster by proposing to transfer his power, and with it his ability to act, to others, though retaining his title, his throne, and his crown. This is a one-way ticket to tragedy; the rest of the drama shows this ruler who would not rule being torn to pieces by the forces he had released. After all, it was his job to govern. This has been implicit in the drama of institutional power, perhaps, since institutions were first formed in the dawn of history. It is, apparently, an essential quality of power itself.

Accurately analyzed, power (as far as it carries) is always absolute. It may be and usually is limited in scope—a quite different proposition. As in the case of the state, the power of corporate management should not be exercised at all, cannot be exercised without penalty, and may be reviewed by extraneous authority, in certain areas. This is a limitation of the field of power. Within those limitations is an enormous field in which managements act in their "discretion"—which is merely a lawyer's way of saying that their power is uncontrolled.

But is there no check, offset, or counterpoise to this

sort of power? With this precise problem we must concern ourselves.

Study of the history of politics—more accurately, of the organization of power—develops in striking repetition the phenomenon of counterpoise. Apparently absolute power in any form of organization is commonly accompanied by the emergence of countervailing power elsewhere in the same organization—usually in quite different form; and the two nuclei of power coexist in opposition to form a balance. Creation of that balance indeed seems to be the fact which preserves the continuity of the power itself. Absolute power unbalanced is anarchic; it eventually destroys both its surroundings and itself. Wise statesmanship from earliest times has recognized and accepted this fact. The history of American common law affords a striking example.

If ever authority was absolute and power unlimited save by physical capacity, the condition existed in England under the early Norman kings. The only real limitation was the danger of successful revolt. Yet from the beginning there was recognition of something intangible demanding to be taken into account. We noted that the subject of a Norman duke, if he could get to the duke's presence, could cry, "Haro," and state whatever grievance he had, even against the duke himself.

The appeal had to be based on the conscience of the duke or king: the appellant had no guarantees in the matter. Yet the ruler, whether for moral or practical considerations, or both combined, considered himself obliged at least to give him consideration. In the earliest days of the English monarchy the king gave more or less ritual form to this: it was called *Aula Regis* ("the King's Great Hall") or, a little later, *Curia Regis*—"the King's Court." Here the Norman or Plantagenet king sits in person among his lords; chief of them is a man (quite often a chaplain or priest) who later comes to be known as "Chancellor." He is the keeper of the conscience of the king. Part of the substantial business of this assembly is to receive petitions—of any and of all kinds. Where appropriate the king is supposed to redress grievance according to his best conscience. As Bracton observed in his review of the Laws and Customs of England, "For the crown of the King is to do justice and judgment, and to maintain peace, and without which the crown cannot exist nor hold." When the king's absolute power was encountering check by the barons at Runnymede in 1215, one grievance was that the *Curia Regis* traveled round with the king who was often in foreign lands, so that his "conscience" could not easily be got at. Wherefore the eleventh chapter of Magna Carta exacted that it should be located "in a certain place." The place decided on was Westminster, and there British courts with equity jurisdiction sit to this day.

Consider, for a moment, this odd emergence of counterpoise to absolute power. The "conscience of the king" had a wide field of responsibility—or perhaps a great accumulation of burdens. The king, like a modern corporation executive, was apt to be occupied. An officer presently emerges with the title of Chancellor, originally more often a bishop than a politician or lawyer. King Henry II, possibly abetted by his wife, the famous Eleanor of Aquitaine, used his conscience to "annul unjust laws, and execute[s] the rightful commands of the pious prince, and put[s] an end to what is injustice to the people or to morals." This was the job of a twelfth-century Chancellor in the time of crusading Richard Lionheart. The interesting question is why an absolute monarchy felt it desirable to work up this sort of device; why, a little later, politically conscious England at Runnymede should have taken steps to assure and institutionalize its continuation. One has leave only to speculate, remembering that the Norman duke had felt similar constraint to answer the "Haro ' cry. Perhaps from that speculation some guide may be reached to certain of the more curious developments in corporation law of today.

Deep in human consciousness is embedded the assumption that somewhere, somehow, there is a higher law which imposes itself in time on princes and powers and institutions of this terrestrial earth. We must leave doctrine to the theologians; but as students of legal history we have to take account of the persistent fact of this huge assumption. Keepers of the tradition of this higher law—medicine men in primitive times, magicians or sybils in the ancient world, or divines today— are regularly listened to with respect. They have power, though it is not the power either of purse or sword. Throughout western history a priest could commonly intimidate a policeman; the Cross could quite frequently stop the king. Failure to satisfy at least a modicum of the demands of this higher law (as they were understood at the time) could weaken materially, or possibly even destroy totally, the effective power of the king and his supporting organization. Wisely, English kings recognized that fact and provided a viable, generally acceptable means of invoking it, and in general complied more or less with current understanding and interpretation of it. Higher law was inchoate—there, but not explicit, to be apprehended and worked out as you went along. Yet its existence was real enough. Violation of it meant trouble. Even a prince who might be skeptical about damnation to hell could understand very well the practical and political dangers of being hated by any inconsiderable sector of his people, not to mention the possibility of his being deposed if an appreciable part of his civil or military organization went looking for a new leader.

It is here suggested that a somewhat similar phenomenon is slowly looming up in the corporate field through the mists that hide from us the history of the next generation. There is beginning to be apparent a realization of a counter force which checks, and remotely acts on, and in time may modify in certain areas the absolute power of business discretion. In our system it emerges in time as law; and good lawyers watch for it.

3

This theory of opposed forces does not accord with some of the recent, more admirable analyses of the American corporation. Mr. Peter Drucker, in the course of abandoning a career of study of philosophy for practice as a managerial consultant, considers that the corporation, as a representative institution, must solve two combined enigmas, both political: that of achieving functional harmony between corporation and society and that of achieving harmony between the corporate activities and prevailing ethical ideas. On analysis, the conception of harmony is hardly the activating principle—harmony is rarely achieved except in heaven or Nirvana, both of which lie beyond the scope of this study. What is actually going on here is rather a process of opposed forces coming into balance. The ethics translated into doctrines and natural law by the Catholic Church in the twelfth century did not "harmonize" with old King Henry II: they checked him. He had brains enough to recognize the fact, so his kingdom attained a degree of internal peace. His son, King John, did not, and the kingdom very nearly broke up. The balance was restored, more or less, when he made terms with the barons.

Some years ago the president and directors of a very powerful life insurance company placed a large contract for advertising and publicity with a small firm organized by the young son of the company's president. Concededly the young man's work was well done. Judgment as to its desirability was fairly within the discretionary powers of the company management: no suggestion was made that the discretion was abused. The fees paid were standard rates prevailing in the business. At the same time certain law firms, members of which sat on the board, were retained to act for the corporation in various matters of importance. The compensation they received was substantial but concededly fair, and the work called for was admittedly required to protect

the interests of the company and its various investments. There was no room for suggestion that the corporation itself or any policy-holder had suffered. But
the Superintendent of Insurance of the State of New
York made an issue on the facts. He insisted that the
directors of the corporation procure the retirement of
the president. Under the rule prevailing in the state
of New York, courts sustain contracts made by a corporation even where the directors and officers are personally interested provided the terms are fair, and the
facts have been fully disclosed. The revealed facts placed
the transaction in question squarely within this rule.

The company's board of directors, faced with this
demand of the Insurance Superintendent, presently
acquiesced. The president, whose quarter-century of
service had been a brilliant success and under whose
guidance the corporation had enormously prospered,
was dealt with by an understanding that he would re-
tire at the next election meeting. Whatever the law,
something more was running here. The board might
have elected to fight it out in the courts (the authority
of the Superintendent in these matters was at least open
to challenge). They might have gone to the newspapers
and fought it out as a quasi-political matter. But the
name of the institution would have been at hazard. The
precise issue would have been whether an executive of

a fiduciary institution such as an insurance company could properly favor his son, even though applicable law would have discovered no damage and would have sanctioned the transaction. Businessmen who are meticulous in handling power are invariably nervous at invoking that power even legitimately when the fact brings disadvantage to their public relations and standing. It is an affair of conscience, sufficiently widely recognized so that one of the most powerful institutions in the United States found it wise not to contest an issue in respect of which they might be found to be conscientiously in the wrong, however right under the law.

Of interest was the fact that companion and competing corporations in this field generally agreed with the decision. An issue was involved and lines of possible conflict drawn in which an obligation based essentially on conscience was likely to crystallize suddenly and sharply into a rigid rule, given form possibly by a court, possibly by legislation, perhaps by an embattled press. The Superintendent of Insurance of the State of New York did not look at all like the keeper of the corporate conscience, nor was he. But he could powerfully insist that the corporation keep its own. He was not even, perhaps, endowed with the power of the state to do anything more than find and state the facts—but that was enough. It is probable that the corporate system in this case was sufficiently safeguarded because someone had the power to find and state the facts, at least to the corporation itself.

But for one corporate situation in which an outside individual or institution can invoke this power, there are hundreds where no such specific *Curia Regis* exists. A very great corporation in the Midwest employs tens of thousands of men in a single city. Its policies and employment are considered as enlightened as those of any comparable concern in the country—perhaps in the world. It maintains in at least one of its divisions an index file of many thousands of names of individuals which it does not wish to employ. This was not wholly its choice. Because like many great corporations, it manufactures armament, it must comply with the so-called "security regulations" of the branch of the Department of Defense with which it contracts. These exact that no one constituting a "security risk" shall be employed in certain sorts of armament manufacture. Enough has been proved of espionage to make it clear that such regulation is not unreasonable. In addition to the list of individuals not considered good security risks, there are also names of men who have been criticized or who may be considered dangerous—or at least whose past actions have been such that the corporation might be criticized if it employed them. An applicant for employment who is a son or a nephew of one of these men, or who gives one of them as reference or otherwise suggests that he is in contact with him, is automatically denied employment. There are other ramifications of the system—a system well enough understood by the personnel departments of many large enterprises.

The existence of such a list is understandable enough. The problem it attempts to meet is clearly and obviously present. Any management given a choice between hiring an employee who might give rise to criticism and one who would not obviously would choose the latter. The power to choose employees in a field not covered by a union contract is absolute. And yet, there is something here which comes within the realms of the corporate conscience. A young man applies for a white-collar job; he is innocent enough to give as reference a teacher who perhaps once interested him and with whom he became acquainted; the teacher is on the list; the young man is denied employment. Especially if the fact of his application and rejection on this ground becomes known, he finds that his whole life is affected and one great avenue of livelihood and occupation is barred to him. His connection with this teacher may have no bearing whatever on his own security status.

This would be the occasion for him to cry, "Haro," demanding that the representative of the power look into the matter and review his case. But there is no one to answer. At long last, of course, he, or enough of him, can band together and in time make such public clamor as they can raise. Possibly in the dim future something might be done about the system—meantime, of course, he would merely advertise and thereby increase his own difficulties. The personnel men with whom he has talked are sympathetic and feel badly about it, but the situation lies beyond their field of competence. If the young man happens by any chance to know the president of the corporation or an influential director, he may find someone who will go into the whole situation, decide that he is not a "security risk," and let him go forward as a matter of accident of contact and frank favor; but this proves nothing except that powerful friends are assets to a career. Somewhere here there is a lacuna in the system of power and it violates conscience and scruple—an institutional failure.

The failure is in not having a keeper of conscience, to whom appeal can be made, by whom inquiry and a fair hearing must be provided, and from whom a humanely fair decision can be had. To a student of law this may be an evil. In any event, to a student of political science it is a weakness and therefore a blunder. In some areas, at least, there is evidence that corporation management is beginning to realize the fact.

4

Thus, in one field the right of appeal against this kind of absolute power (if it is absolute) is beginning to be recognized by custom. Let us take the very unromantic level of the dealer-distributor who sells the product of the large corporation.

We must approach this group of people with more respect than is presently accorded salesmen in current literature. There are, for example, about 47,000 dealer-agents of automobiles in the United States; the largest single group of these naturally are the agents of the so-called "Big Three" motor corporations—General Motors, Ford, and Chrysler. It is not easy to calculate the total capital assets of this group. General Motors requires that any dealer-agent appointed by it shall have a minimum capital, said to be about $100,000. One may hazard the estimate that the total assets of automobile dealer-agents in the United States aggregate more than three billion dollars—probably a good deal more than that. They are also the nuclei of business and organization in every substantial town in the country. The shop, garage, service facilities, and so forth, grouped around the businessman who has the Ford agency, the Chrysler agency, or the General Motors agency are familiar and substantial elements of American business.

The basis of the position of each of these dealer-agents is a "contract," frequently known as a franchise, with the automobile corporation whose cars he sells. The contract itself is a framework rather than a definition. Under it, there is a general understanding that the company will sell to the dealer; the dealer will buy cars from the company for resale. No fixed number of cars are mentioned; the wholesale and retail prices are to be fixed from time to time; the dealer is not "bound" to buy the cars and resell them (though, of course, he is out of business if he does not); the company has quite ample escape clauses so that it does not need to deliver cars to him. The dealer is not "the agent" and certainly not the employee of the company. In effect, a loose relationship is established.

The "contract" is cancelable. Some companies permit cancellation at will by either side. Others permit cancellation on ninety days' notice. For practical purposes, the company has the overriding position. After a contract is canceled, the dealer's investment in good will, advertising, sales arrangements, servicing facilities, and so forth, goes by the board. Cancellation by the company may easily put him out of business: it would not be simple for him to get another agency. Against this must be set the fact that the companies themselves rely in large measure on their "dealer relationships." Cancellation of a dealership makes ill will in the community, frightens other dealers, and if resorted to arbitrarily will adversely affect sales. Everything considered, however, the preponderance of power is overwhelmingly on the side of the company.

The company can, accordingly, fix what amount or quota of cars the dealer must sell. These may, and frequently do, include new types of cars which the community service does not particularly want and which the dealer finds it difficult to dispose of. To secure the necessary number of four-door sedans which perhaps are readily salable, he may have to order a couple of pick-up trucks, station wagons, or two-tone convertibles, which his constituency does not take. Since the dealer has to pay cash outright, this amounts to a real burden and frequently to a considerable risk. If he is unable to dispose of a particular type of car before a new model is announced, he may find himself in very bad shape indeed. He is accordingly under pressure and his business policies must conform more or less to that pressure. The extreme penalty of failure to conform is loss of the contract, and corresponding, often crushing, loss of investment and business status. Less extreme penalty may be failure to secure full allotment of readily salable vehicles, diminishing the dealer's possible profit. The apparent legal relationship is such that the dealer has no enforcible rights; in any case the economic relationship is such that he cannot afford to quarrel.

And yet, in the presence of this power a limiting custom has grown up. The extreme penalty—cancellation of contract—is not normally invoked by the company except for cause, such as bankruptcy, extreme misconduct of the dealer, attempt to assign the contract, or the like. Where it is imposed, General Motors, for one, has established an administrative board of review. A dealer whose contract is canceled is given the right to appeal against the cancellation; the board accords him a hearing at which the dealer may show that the action is unjustifiable; and the board may reverse the cancellation. So it seems that in this relationship at least the lacuna in the system—the need of a *Curia Regis* to give effect to the conscience of the king—is beginning to be filled in.

There are, of course, important defects in this arrangement. Appeal from company action is a matter of grace and not of right—but then, appeal to the *Curia Regis* and the exercise of the conscience of the king also was originally a matter of grace. It is of interest that in at least one state—Rhode Island—the right granted by General Motors has crystallized into explicit statute law. Under the Rhode Island legislation, cancellation of an agency may be appealed to a state administrative board, and the board after review may reverse the cancellation and direct that the relationship be restored.

This homely illustration perhaps sufficiently indicates the existence of a principle of far wider application. A habit of mind crystallizing into a commercial custom which can demand review of the power of cancellation of an agency contract, apparently prevails outside the automobile business. It was reported some time ago that a dealer in General Electric products publicly questioned the right of General Electric to terminate a dealer relationship with that company. One would expect to find a trend toward limitation on arbitrary power gradually appearing through the entire field— whether it concern franchises granted by Coca-Cola to a manufacturer-salesman, or dealer-company relationships prevailing between farm machinery companies and their outlets, or other like arrangements through the entire range.

Tiny though the indication may be, it indicates a tropism in the emerging American corporate system.

Power to deal at will with other men's property and occupation, however absolute it may be as a matter of technical contract law, is subject to certain limitations. They still lie in the field of inchoate law: we are not as yet able to cite explicit case and statute law clearly stating these limitations. We can only say that in this field a matrix of equity jurisdiction is beginning to appear.

Probably it is not accidental that it begins to be visible in the dealer-company relationship field, though in and of itself abuse of power in that area is less humanly poignant than in the field of employment and human relations. A dealer must put up money—and hazard that. He must invest his time, his business activity, and his business name—and hazard that. On the property side, the power of the company includes, virtually, though not legally, the power to destroy part, if not all, of this investment. The dealer is closer to the grass-roots of a community than is the company, perhaps distantly situated in Detroit or elsewhere, and a wrong done to him injures the public relations of the company. The Norman peasant who considered himself wronged might be disregarded as an individual, but if there were any considerable number of him, the duke had trouble on his hands in Rouen or Falaise or Caen—and that kind of trouble had a way of spreading.

Common sense and sound government dictated accordingly that the situation be met in terms roughly satisfactory to the community. So, apparently, the duke satisfied the problem by an act of grace which was also an act of morality as well as of common sense and enlightened self-interest. Presently, as a custom of the realm, that particular form of grace became a right, institutionalized to provide more or less predictable remedies.

We have been considering the corporate system as a form of political organization. The rules of successful political organization have exhibited a degree of uniformity throughout the history of the western world. Is it far-fetched to predict that the rules applicable to power in a political state will reappear in modified dress when power centralizes itself around a politico-economic instead of a governmental institution?

5

The General Electric Company is, justly, one of the most respected of American corporations. Its management has been able and of unquestioned integrity. Its material success has been great. Its scientific and technical experimental work has been outstanding. It has been selected by the Defense Department of the government of the United States to manufacture vast amounts of defense material. Even more important, it has been entrusted with development of a number of new applications of science which may revolutionize American production. So, it has had the "developmental orders" for jet engines, and has a lead in that crucial field, and is also pioneering at least one great phase of the use of atomic energy to provide power—to name only two of the many projects on which it works. In the course of this work it has come under the security regulations of the Department of Defense.

In the closing months of 1953, a Senate Committee, following various leads, elected to investigate the personnel of two of its plants. It was said, perhaps accurately, that some of the men working in them were, or at all events had been, Communists. In the ensuing hearings, some of the employees subpoenaed for investigation, refused to answer questions, pleading privilege against self-incrimination. Presently the president, Mr. Ralph J. Cordiner, announced that anyone refusing to answer questions on this ground in a General Electric plant, or any individual who, being accused of Communism, refused to answer questions on plea of privilege against self-incrimination, would be suspended. Presumably, if proved to be a Communist, he would be discharged.

Given the international situation, the overtly hostile

attitude of the Soviet government, and the undeniable fact that American Communists are, in large measure, if not wholly, controlled by the desires and instructions of the Soviet government, the policy was fully understandable. Comment on Mr. Cordiner's action was almost universally favorable—with a few exceptions. Notable among these was the editorial position of the *Berkshire Eagle,* an outstanding Republican newspaper published at Pittsfield in western Massachusetts in which General Electric has important plants. The editor of the *Eagle* asked a couple of pertinent questions. How is the right of an individual to be protected in case he is accused of Communism? Does he have privilege against self-incrimination or not? It is all right, perhaps, to discharge a Communist; but is the action taken on evidence, or on someone's hunch? Is a man discharged because he is really a Communist, or because someone accuses him of Communism, or because he once was a Communist in his college days? And how do you know? Is the individual involved to be given the chance to refute the accusation? In such a proceeding does he have counsel, constitutional privilege against self-incrimination or not? In other words, is there any requirement of due process of law in this business, or are we in a field of arbitrary power?

The questions raised by the *Berkshire Eagle* were

not technically put, but they raised a whole complex of problems in a single package. Sorting them out,

First: The General Electric is a private corporation. Subject to any labor contracts it may have, it has the right to hire and fire at will. It need give no reasons. It may simply decide that Nym and Bardolph and Pistol (to give Shakespearean names to our accused) are characters they do not want in their plants. Equally, in theory, it could decide that card-carrying members of the Democratic Party ought not to be encouraged to reside in Lynn or Pittsfield, Massachusetts, or Schenectady, New York, the General Electric being the preponderant employer in all three cities, and therefore ought not to be employed. This is the straight exercise of rights of private property and of private management, and is generally accepted by the law. Does this right need to be brought up for re-examination?

Second: The General Electric, as an employer, has no particular objections to Nym, Bardolph, and Pistol. But it does have extensive business relationships with the government of the United States. A Senate committee singles out Nym, Bardolph, and Pistol, alleging that they are Communists, that they are opposing the United States government, and that they are potential material for sabotage or espionage. Because the three refuse to incriminate themselves on Constitutional grounds, they are plain targets for criticism which involves the General Electric. Under this pressure, General Electric thereupon discharges the men, and forbids their further employment at any of its establishments, plants or other installations which actually exist in some ninety cities. This is the exercise of the General Electric's private right to hire and fire at will, but under visible pressure of an arm of the United States government.

Third: General Electric has contracts to produce goods and do work for the Department of Defense of the United States. Included in their contracts is a clause requiring the corporation to comply with regulations designed to safeguard "security"—that is, to protect the operations against possible sabotage and to prevent information concerning them from falling into unauthorized hands. Under the clause, security authorities or other appropriate officers of the Department of Defense can designate individuals whom they regard as insecure, and perhaps designate categories of individuals, similarly so regarded, the General Electric agreeing that it will eliminate such people on request. They designate Nym, Bardolph, and Pistol as "security risks," whereupon the men are discharged. In this case, the General Electric has agreed to exercise its power to hire and fire in accordance with directions of a department of the Federal government, and on government direction has terminated the employment and employability of the three men.

At this point lawyers and students of the legal system are bound to take account of the problem.

We may begin by sympathizing with Mr. Cordiner—and perhaps also with the security officers of the Defense Department. Mr. Cordiner is responsible for the direction of General Electric, which includes responsibility for its public relations—which, as we have seen, are of first importance. In addition, he has to think of the business and profit-making interest of his company, of which defense contracts are a very substantial element. Substantial indeed in more ways than would appear, for not only does the General Electric make a profit on its defense orders, but it also thereby secures an immense lead in knowledge of new techniques not otherwise available. He may have the greatest desire in the world to assure exact justice to Nym, Bardolph, and Pistol. But he has to balance their interests against the interests of the company, and perhaps also the interests of the United States. No bed of roses certainly; the safest thing to do is to sacrifice the individuals, since he clearly runs the least chance of trouble that way than by taking any other course.

We can also understand the feeling of the men in the

headline that particular company. What was needed was a proper government policy which would both protect the rights of individuals against false accusations and eliminate danger from known subversives. In blunt, they wanted the government to take over the job.

Analyzing the problem presented, it is perfectly clear that General Electric was right. It had power—which it had not sought. Problems were thrust upon it of a governmental order. If government in this respect did not occupy the territory and govern, General Electric had to do so; the fault lay with the government for not moving in. Examination of the applicable considerations fully bears this out.

Sorting out the three problems, we may tackle them in inverse order. To begin, let us deal with a situation in which a powerful corporation is under a contract duty to the United States government, or some agency of it, to fire or decline to hire individuals designated to them as possible security risks. In practice they mean that a man who may have been employed for years, being suspect for some reason, is designated to the appropriate authorities in General Electric. Things then happen to him rapidly. All he knows is that he is called into the office one day and told that he is discharged— or at best transferred to some far less desirable job.

field of security relations, the function of establishing categories of unemployables and of determining what individuals fell within them was no job whatever for a private corporation. In an *Employee Relations News Letter* issued on March 4, 1954, they forcefully called attention to the fact that five times in recent years the General Electric had urged on a Congressional committee the need for new security legislation. The company rightly insisted that government, not private citizens, must identify traitors—and that this government duty could not safely or properly be left to private citizens. They repeated requests previously made that the government—presumably under appropriate Congressional authority—should determine and direct when an employee should be excluded from employment by General Electric, because

employers and defense contractors cannot and should not be expected to embark privately upon sweeping programs for judging the loyalty of employees. In the very nature of the problem, such action might compel them to make discharges based upon suspicions and rumors which the employer would be in no position to authoritatively evaluate or prove.

They added that the security problems of General Electric were essentially the same as those of many other firms and that it was out of all proportion to under law they would have swung for it in a county jail: the lynch mob is nonetheless guilty of murder and worse. It is guilty of a violation of public order. As noted, the comparison is unfair because in the case of the lynch mob there is a perfectly clear system of law and of established public order, and the remedy of the lynchers obvious in the extreme: they could ring up the local police and let the law take its course. Mr. Cordiner unhappily was acting in a field where there is no such clear law, and he had to do the best he could. Under the circumstances he made some himself, at least as far as his power over General Electric affairs carried, and here the issue is joined. Lawyers and students of political science now have to pick up the discussion, looking toward the day (one hopes swiftly to come) when there will be recognized law, and a recognized system of public order, and a clear line of action for the head of a great corporation. Apparently it is as necessary to the health of Mr. Cordiner's organization as it was to the organization of old Duke Rollo or of William the Conqueror.

Because we have used Mr. Cordiner and General Electric as an illustrative case, the record should be completed to be fully fair to them. No one realized better than they the nature of these questions. The General Electric was rigorous in feeling that, in the particular

Defense Department responsible for security of defense production, and particularly of secret operations. Their job is getting the work done, and keeping information about it where it belongs. Most of us know enough about organized Communists to know that they are hostile to the national interests of the United States, to the company interests of General Electric, and to the freedoms that most of us hold dear. We may agree that it might well be reasonable to have laws placing Communists in a special category, and that it might be reasonable exercise of legislative power to exclude that category from employment in plants engaged in defense production. And yet, when this is said, somehow the questions raised by the *Berkshire Eagle* (in which, to its credit, the *Providence Journal* presently joined) have still not been answered. Something is wrong with the picture.

The obtrusive fact is that we do not clearly see "law" here at all, let alone "due process of law." Though the comparison is odious and wholly unjust to Mr. Cordiner, blanket action by a dominant power is a little too much like lynch law. Suppose Nym and his two friends were in fact Communists. No one ever yet justified or validated the action of a lynch mob by proving that the men it hung were actually guilty of crime. Assume that they were: and that by proper prosecution partment of the Federal government, and on government direction has terminated the employment and employability of the three men.

At this point lawyers and students of the legal system are bound to take account of the problem.

We may begin by sympathizing with Mr. Cordiner—and perhaps also with the security officers of the Defense Department. Mr. Cordiner is responsible for the direction of General Electric, which includes responsibility for its public relations—which, as we have seen, are of first importance. In addition, he has to think of the business and profit-making interest of his company, of which defense contracts are a very substantial element. Substantial indeed in more ways than would appear, for not only does the General Electric make a profit on its defense orders, but it also thereby secures an immense lead in knowledge of new techniques not otherwise available. He may have the greatest desire in the world to assure exact justice to Nym, Bardolph, and Pistol. But he has to balance their interests against the interests of the company, and perhaps also the interests of the United States. No bed of roses certainly; the safest thing to do is to sacrifice the individuals, since he clearly runs the least chance of trouble that way than by taking any other course.

We can also understand the feeling of the men in the

grounds, they are plain targets for criticism which involves the General Electric. Under this pressure, General Electric thereupon discharges the men, and forbids their further employment at any of its establishments, plants or other installations which actually exist in some ninety cities. This is the exercise of the General Electric's private right to hire and fire at will, but under visible pressure of an arm of the United States government.

Third: General Electric has contracts to produce goods and do work for the Department of Defense of the United States. Included in their contracts is a clause requiring the corporation to comply with regulations designed to safeguard "security"—that is, to protect the operations against possible sabotage and to prevent information concerning them from falling into unauthorized hands. Under the clause, security authorities or other appropriate officers of the Department of Defense can designate individuals whom they regard as insecure, and perhaps designate categories of individuals, similarly so regarded, the General Electric agreeing that it will eliminate such people on request. They designate Nym, Bardolph, and Pistol as "security risks," whereupon the men are discharged. In this case, the General Electric has agreed to exercise its power to hire and fire in accordance with directions of a de-

If the ban is complete, and he lives in any of the cities in which the corporation is a preponderant employer, the consequences are extreme. The main avenue of employment is closed to him. He must move into some other city and find some other job if he can. Since the same ban will probably follow him into any other plant engaged in defense orders, the going is rough. If he is a young man, he winds up in some recognizably marginal job, such as dishwashing or unskilled labor. If he is a man in middle life, he may end on the industrial scrap heap. Probably he never discovers exactly what hit him. The personnel people of the corporations do not confide to him their reasons for action.

The young man applying for a job referred to above is in an exactly similar situation.

The individual goes through a harrowing time, especially if he knows, suspects, or finds out (as he usually does) via the grapevine, the gist of what is going on. He may have every reason to consider that he is entirely innocent of wrongdoing—as indeed frequently he is. He may be quite convinced that certain kinds of conduct, including membership in the Communist Party, or conscious participation in a subversive group, would make him ineligible for certain kinds of employment. The difficulty is that he did none of these things. Someone proscribed him because they considered that there was a degree of probability that he might have been or later might be guilty of the forbidden conduct. So he goes from pillar to post, trying to find someone who will listen to his story—but there is no one to listen. Then he begins to ask questions about the whole system. By whose authority, and under what color of law, has this particular kind of conduct resulted in so grave a penalty? What procedure establishes guilt or innocence, when the conduct is charged? There is no one to answer these questions either. And so a mounting wave of frustrated protest grows. It has become a national problem.

In the case we have been discussing, the corporation acted as undisclosed agent or agency of a branch of the Federal government. Though the power it exercised is its own, it was exercised at the direction of a Federal official. At this point, to a lawyer, it would seem that the Fifth Amendment to the Constitution of the United States becomes squarely applicable—and not the part about self-incrimination either. The Amendment reads: "No person shall be . . . deprived of life, liberty or property without due process of law." The ten amendments were, of course, adopted, as the Preamble to them recites, "to prevent misconstruction or abuse of its (the Government's Constitutional) powers," and they related to acts of the Federal government.

Our corporation in the case supposed acted nominally by private right but actually because a branch of the Federal government required it so to act. The results have been grave. The right to continued employment is unquestionably a property right; the right to get employment freely is, if not a property right, at least a substantial part of liberty. Both have been impaired, and both at the instance of the government, though the agency is a private corporation and the enforcement is carried out through its personnel and hiring officers without displaying United States marshals' badges.

Was there "due process of law"? Three elements enter into due process. The first is that some valid law exists under which the action was taken, enacted by competent authority—in the case of the Federal government, the Congress of the United States. Within limits, the Congress may delegate administrative powers; it is possible that it might validly delegate administrative power to the security officers of the Defense Department to determine categories of individuals who might be deemed "security risks." Such an act of Congress, or administrative action taken thereunder, can be tested in the courts to determine whether it violates the Constitutional limitations. For instance, a Federal law or administrative action barring Catholics as such from

95

defense plants would be, *ipso facto,* violative of the First Amendment. Yet in the case supposed it is current practice—no showing whatever is made of authority to enact the rule relied on resulting in discharge or unemployability.

Without such authority, the Federal government has no more right to demand that the General Electric discharge the three men than you or I might have. Nor can it enlarge its power by any form of contract it may exact from General Electric or any other corporation. All it can do by that is to get General Electric into trouble.

But let us assume that there is statute law setting up a category of unemployables—or, if you like, statutory authority granting to the Defense Department or other agency of the United States administrative power to set up such a category. Let us further assume that this authority has been well exercised—that is, that the statute or the administrative authority delegated by the statute meets the tests and requirements of the Constitution of the United States. Let us further make the assumption (though justification for it is far from clear) that an agency of the Federal government could, by contract, set up the contracting corporation as undisclosed instrumentality to enforce the statutory policy—that is, to deny employment to individuals falling within the proscribed group. It will be seen that these assumptions are violent. The Constitution severely limits the power of Congress along these lines. Legislation prohibiting the employment of Catholic or Protestant or Jew in defense plants would almost certainly violate the First Amendment to the Constitution as an abridgment of freedom of religion. There is severe limitation on the power of Congress to delegate authority of this kind to an administrative agency, say the Defense Department, the Foreign Operations Administration, or the like. Standards for the use of delegated authority must be carefully laid down. Administrative authority so exercised must be within the prescribed standards, and reasonably adapted to accomplish the Congressional purpose; and so forth. For the sake of argument let us go on the assumption that all is in order. But all we have got, thus far, is "law." We still have not got "due process of law." For Nym, Bardolph, and Pistol have a clear Constitutional right to insist that the penalties set up shall not be applied to them unless they are shown to fall within the proscribed category. Some sort of fact-determining procedure must be open to them. But of this, in the case stated, and in thousands of cases like it, there has not been the faintest glimmer of adequate attempt to satisfy the requirements of "due process."

The Congress of the United States could not pass an act stating that Nym, Bardolph, and Pistol should henceforth be ineligible for employment in any plant having a defense order: that would be a legislative finding of guilt, unconstitutional as a Bill of Attainder under Article I of the Federal Constitution. Nor could Congress delegate to an administrative agency any similar power. Still less, it would seem, can it require a private corporation contracting with it to execute a nominally private Bill of Attainder by putting Nym, Bardolph, and Pistol on a list of unemployables. And if any officer of the Federal government undertook to do so, or if a corporation undertook to do so on behalf of or at the insistence of an agency of the Federal government, that corporation would seem to be liable to the men injured.

For at this point another doctrine of Constitutional law enters the picture. A government officer who acts unconstitutionally in carrying out his office ceases to be an officer of the government and becomes an individual. He becomes personally liable to the individual aggrieved. In vain the official pleads that he was doing the government's work, that he was not acting personally, that the complaint ought to run against the government itself. Our Constitutional law coolly, cruelly, but correctly and therapeutically rejects the argument.

It says that if he acted unconstitutionally he stepped outside the protection of his governmental office, and that it is he, John Doe, who committed the act, and is therefore liable for damages in case the act is found illegal. This would seem to be the position of a corporation which discharges men in conformity with a clause in a government contract—if it be found that the direction given to it by the government agency was given without valid authority, or that procedure in applying it violates due process of law. Bluntly, the employing corporation may be liable in an action for damages, depending on whether arbitrary action dictated under the security clause is found within or without the "due process" clause of the Fifth Amendment. Damages might be considerable. In Pittsfield, Massachusetts, or Schenectady, New York, where General Electric is far and away the largest employer, in Fort Dearborn or Detroit, Michigan, where General Motors and Ford are overwhelmingly the chief employers, denial of right to work for these companies may be equivalent to denial of livelihood in a man's home town. To say that his "liberty or property" has been taken from him is no legalistic figure of speech. It is a literal fact.

All other questions are grimly material. Arbitrary determination that such-and-such person is insecure will not do: the day might come when in a Democratic

Administration every Republican is deemed arbitrarily to be insecure; or in a Republican Administration that every Democrat is *ipso facto* insecure. Or, if you like, when religious controversy runs high, that a Protestant should not be employed for reasons of "insecurity"; or perhaps a Mormon. Already in one government department its security officer objected to the presence of a Quaker as officer of a private organization considered for contract work—as flagrant a violation of American tradition as can well be imagined. Interruption of existing employment relationship or denial of the opportunity, if not the right, to work for an employer willing to hire, can be justified only on the ground that a state of facts exists under which the employment endangers the carrying out of a legitimate public purpose. Any other rule leads straight to totalitarianism—which Americans thus far have never tolerated, and which businessmen have always, and rightly, resisted.

Fairness requires appreciative reference to the painstaking and conscientious efforts of some government departments—notably the Department of Defense—to meet the issue. The problem arose in many forms. The eligibility of some company to receive defense contracts might be called in question on "security grounds." Committees of the Defense Department have been set up to deal with such cases, with rudimentary statement of charge, opportunity to file answer, and the naming of a Board to hear any defense the company might present. Infinitely more numerous are cases in which the availability of a particular individual for employ- ment is brought into question. The range is wide: an individual in a given employment may require access to "classified information." Or he may be at work or pro- posed for work in some operation in respect of which secrecy is enjoined. There, the Department has set up an "Industrial Personnel Security Board" with regional offices in various parts of the country. These Boards have screening committees reviewing derogatory infor- mation in respect of an individual. They apprise him of the fact that his employment may not be "clearly consistent" with the policy of the government, and the reasons why, and offer him a chance to file an answer. If the answer does not dispose of the matter to the satisfaction of the committee, he may then request a hearing and present evidence.

In the writer's experience, these Boards have been composed of conscientious and careful men. Within the limitations imposed on them, they have endeavored to be fair and understanding. More than one individual has gone into the procedure believing that he would not have just treatment, and has come out with his faith in American humanity restored. But it is still true that the individual must disprove the charge made against him. Proof of any indictment, like the source of it, is secret; the witness for the prosecution never appears. The point must be made, however, that the Department of Defense has not ignored the problem and within its limitations has made a praiseworthy attempt to meet it. Unfortunately it must be added that the procedure does not cover the entire field and probably cannot; and that many departments of the government have not done nearly as well as has the United States Army.

Thus far we have been considering the power of the corporation to decree and inflict unemployability under influence or compulsion of contract with the Federal government. It remains to glance briefly at the problem where the same measures are taken by the corporation on its own behalf, without reference to any government contract or pressure. The problem here is more difficult, and the area uncharted. The constitutional right on which the previous argument is based is an individual's right under the American Constitution not to have his government deprive him of liberty or property without due process. The effect of government contract or other pressure substantially converts a corporation into a government agency, and its acts into a government act, and we have a constitutional principle for guide. But suppose there is no underlying contract, and there is no government pressure: the corporation, considering its operations and the public interest, makes a rule proscribing as unemployable Communists or persons accused of Communism who take refuge behind the privilege against self-incrimination. Has an individual affected by such a rule any rights?

In classical theory, he does not. The business corporation has discretionary power (subject to the limitations imposed by a few Fair Employment Practices Acts in some states) to select and reject employees at will, as a part of the kit of rights going with private property and management power. Yet the classic theory seems somehow not satisfactory. It was made for a time when there were many thousands of employers, and the act and policy of the most powerful of them could relate only to a tiny fragment of the economic complex. The same act or policy carried out by one or two large corporations, controlling a substantial percentage of the employment in a region or industry, has a vastly different effect. In 1804, or even in 1854, the net impact of any corporation policy on the liberty or property of individuals was usually negligible. Under the degree of corporate concentration prevailing in 1954, it may amount to substantial deprivation of opportunity to earn a living. In a companion situation, for instance, few would deny that a policy adopted by a few great gasoline distributing companies to refuse to sell gasoline to Negroes would result quite simply in denying to Negroes the free use of automobiles in that area. Not many would uphold the power of a corporation to do this. So few, in fact, that no large corporation so far as the writer knows has ever considered the possibility. But is there any real difference when it comes to employment?

The corporation is, in theory at least, a creature of the state which charters it, and its operations are sanctioned and in measure aided by any state in which it is authorized to do business. Historically there is sound basis for insisting that the corporation has some color of state authority, its creation being in furtherance of state encouragement of commerce and industry. Corporate action therefore may in the not distant future be held to be controlled by the provisions of the Fourteenth Amendment, which forbids any state government (or anyone acting for such a government) from taking life, liberty, or property from any individual without due process. Where the corporation is actually working under state regulation, as in the case of a public utility, or enjoys some specific state privilege, the tie-up between corporate and state authority becomes clear.

In any event, technicality aside, the fact is that the large corporation is relied upon as a source of supply and goods and services by the organized community. If it has power to use, and does use its supply or employment functions to effect political policies as well as to produce and distribute electricity or gasoline, motor cars or washing machines, it has, *de facto* at least, invaded the political sphere and has become in fact, if not in theory, a quasi-governing agency. The actual step of applying constitutional limitations to corporations as such—where their power effectively impairs "liberty" or takes "property"—has not yet been taken by the courts though the Supreme Court has come within a biscuit-toss of doing so in a couple of cases, notably *Marsh v. Alabama.* Elsewhere, the writer has made the argument that when the case is squarely presented, the courts will cross the line, when it is made to appear that the corporation in fact has power, and in fact has used that power, without due process, in such manner as in fact to deprive an American of liberty or property or other Constitutional rights.

The danger is the ancient one of irresponsible power, functioning outside the discipline of law implicit under organized government. Because the issue arose over Communists, who are deservedly unpopular, its real nature has not been clearly apprehended. Vigilante groups which summarily hung horse thieves may have executed a very desirable policy. The trouble was that they might any day take it into their heads to hang or drive out poets, political opponents, aliens, or men and women whose religion the community disliked. The state of Illinois in 1954 is not proud of the self-appointed community guardian groups which massacred the Mormons at Nauvoo and drove them westward to Utah—though unquestionably proscription of Mormons was popular at the time.

The field whose expanse we have been exploring offers, I suggest, a clear opportunity for legislation. True, the long evolution of constitutional law through court decision as courts are appealed to in one or another case will probably cover the territory in fullness of time. But test cases are difficult and expensive, and while they are being awaited and carried forward, thousands of individuals may suffer bitterly. Some sort of modern civil rights act, setting up a forum to which prompt and effective recourse may be had, seems clearly indicated. If General Electric or General Motors or International Harvester were to imprison a man, writ of *habeas corpus* would lie at once. Because in modern practice a man's liberty may be impaired without seizing his body, rather by cutting off his opportunity to work, the historic writ of *habeas corpus* no longer fits.

But surely an equivalent writ, directing a corporation to show cause why a man has been declared unemployable, could be worked out. The drafting of Federal and state statutes to this end would call for a certain amount of ingenuity and solid measure of historical perspective. But lawyers should be equal to that task—just as the state of Rhode Island was equal to the task of exacting a review when an automobile dealer's agency was summarily canceled.

Pending legislation, it is suggested that corporations themselves are not wholly without capacity to act. They, in respect of their own operations, can erect their own *Aula Regis,* and wisdom would suggest that they do. When Mr. Cordiner or anyone in his position is asked to fire a man on the ground that his conduct makes him unfit for employment, it would be a protection to him to have a procedure worked out. This might be the setting up, by the corporation itself, of a review board, before which a prompt and open hearing could be had, and to which might be referred any charges against any individual employed or seeking employment. They might be irresponsible—brought up by Senator McCarthy, or by the local post of Veterans of Foreign Wars, or some complaining citizens. Or, for that matter, charges by the security officer of the Department of Defense or the personnel people of the corporation's own department. The individual charged should have defined charges, prompt notice, and opportunity to reply. The accuser who had taken it upon himself to file charges could bring forth substantiating evidence, if he had any. More often than not this would be the end of irresponsible accusations: individuals expected to substantiate charges are rather careful about bringing them. If substance was there and defense inadequate, the corporation would have an impartial determination of fact, on the basis of which it could safely exercise its power to retain or discharge an employee. It could indicate with some precision the categories of conduct which it considered as rendering men unemployable; and establish a method of fact-finding, giving reasonable opportunity for determination whether the employee concerned fell within them.

The missing and essential requirement is that the facts justifying proscription be established. Many of us might agree that a ruling requiring discharge of Communists from plants engaged in national defense work is justifiable. We would still insist that the fact of Communism (or other disqualifying conduct) must be sufficiently demonstrated. By settled legal construction this means (a) that a charge must be stated with sufficient definiteness so that the individual has a right to know the charge and can gather and adduce evidence in his own defense; (b) that a hearing shall be had at which the charged person can be represented by counsel; (c) that he may have witnesses in his defense; and (d) that a finding of fact shall be made by a presumptively impartial official or board. It is the writer's belief that such finding, when made, can be reviewed in a Federal court. It is only a question of time before a test case establishes both the necessity of due process prior to discharge and the right of judicial review thereafter.

6

One needs no gift of prophecy to know that in these matters we stand on the threshold of things to come.

Let us project a little the operations of twentieth-century capitalism. Increasingly, the development is toward a mixed system in which governmental and private property are inextricably mingled. This is not the result of any creeping socialism. Rather it is a direct consequence of galloping capitalism.

An outstanding example is the aircraft production industry. Ninety-five per cent of its product is bought by the United States government. An undisclosed but very large percentage of the technical work and resulting patents, processes, know-how, and so forth, is the direct product of work in governmental laboratories or produced by research departments of universities under government contract. It is possible that in the aircraft industry there are men who could sort out the principles, processes, and mechanical developments resulting from private research, and set them apart from those developed and owned by the government of the United States, though this is doubtful. It is almost certain that if such division were made, no modern airplane could be built without drawing heavily on both categories. Even the plants are themselves mixed government and private property: one stand of buildings will have been built by Pratt-Whitney or United Aircraft, while the factories immediately next door, possibly housing part of the same production line, will belong to the United States government though leased to the company. Flow of production is chiefly against government contract—contracts capable of being canceled at will or on relatively short notice. The industry in a word is built on a mixed base, and is likely to operate from that base in the foreseeable future. The companies through their directors and officers can fight for position, demand consideration of their point of view, and indeed can frequently prevail in agreement with the government. But the ultimate power depends on the officers of the United States who plan for air defense, though they in turn are limited by the fact that they must use the principal privately owned aircraft production plants if they are to succeed. So it occurs that in this industry, one of the largest in the United States, there is no clear line between a governmental operation and a private business transaction, no likelihood that such a line will be drawn—or, indeed, that anyone wants to draw it.

The situation in the aircraft industry appears to be merely earnest of more sweeping changes. If General Electric or Westinghouse succeed in solving the problem of making nuclear fission into a source of commercially usable power, the United States government, represented by the Atomic Energy Commission, and at least two of the largest corporations in the country, become virtual partners. There is no objection to this. It results from the fact that in our explosive naissance of scientific development, government happens to play as large a part as does private capitalist enterprise. The scientific heritage of our generation is anything but private in any case; it is the aggregate of the work of generations. No property mark is engraved on most of it. Scientists know better than anyone else that practical developments arising from their research subsume a great range of effort, academic, commercial, governmental, gathered together in the various enterprises afoot. American capitalism in the twentieth century is perhaps the most daring in history, but even it could not assume the unlimited risk and the enormous expense of the Manhattan Project. The development of atomic energy, perhaps the crest of the next great wave in modern development, was not socialist by theory or by design. It was twentieth-century capitalism in respect of which the government played a major part, as it will continue to do.

In this future picture of a vista of capitalism ahead, we cannot grant either to government or to private corporations the individual and arbitrary power thought proper and necessary to the small private entrepreneurs of yesterday. The right of a private individual to run his own business, translated into government, would be intolerable tyranny. Equally, the arbitrariness of government interacting on private capitalism in this mixed system which we are erecting and from which we see no present escape, would reduce private enterprise to a variety of irresponsible socialist bureaucracy. To require hundreds of thousands, perhaps millions, of individuals, to live under a system which translates into government action the uncontrolled individual will of a small-scale private owner would be to change the entire form of American life.

Will we, nill we, there is no escape from looking within as well as without the evolving system. There is no safety save in assuring that the Anglo-American rights in defense of personality, first forged by growing democracy in the teeth of the feudal system, are maintained in the context of the great and powerful corporate institutions emerging as science and government combine to exploit vast new areas in mechanics and economics.

So we return to our Norman duke. We find his modern counterpart and representatives of it in a dozen posts. One may be the director of personnel of a great corporation. Another may be the vice-president in charge of sales, providing for the distribution of his product through sales agencies. A third may be a conscientious and troubled security officer acting for the United States government, giving directions to a corporate contractor. Again, it may be contracting officer of a defense agency, giving or withholding contracts for aircraft, for atomic energy development, for jet engines, for electronics, or what have you. The language of old-style, nineteenth-century capitalism, gives all these, apparently, unlimited power. But each of us knows, and the public knows, that there can be no such thing as unlimited power within the American constitutional system—that system which produced and in turn is the chief framework of twentieth-century capitalism.

So, it seems, the corporations have a conscience, or else accept direction from the conscience of the government. This conscience must be built into institutions so that it can be invoked as a right by the individuals and interests subject to the corporate power. It may not be christened with a Latin name; its keeper may not be called "Chancellor," the place where the conscience can be called into action will no longer be called the *Curia Regis*. But, as at Runnymede through Magna Carta, it will be required to be present and reachable. It will be required to observe certain rules designed for the protection of individuals. The first ten Amendments to the Constitution of the United States—the Bill of Rights —which came down from Magna Carta, which in turn came down from the *Curia Regis* had their remote origin in the same forces which permitted a Norman peasant to stand in the way of the duke and cry, "Haro!"

For twentieth-century capitalism will justify itself not only by its out-turn product, but by its content of life values. Within its organization and impact are lives of many millions of men; and these lives are the first concern, not the by-product, of our century. In American thought, an economic system, like a political government, is made for men. If it denies rights of men to life as they understand life, or to liberty as they understand that, or to property, whatever modern property shall turn out to be, the community gathers itself for a kind of revolt whose results are unforeseeable. Happily the long tradition of the common law and of the American Constitution offers a conception, a means of approach, and a group of institutions making it possible to protect and develop this content. Power of any organization, corporate or governmental, is subject always to judgment by that criterion; and the political effects of community judgments are apt, in the long run, to be decisive.

Bracton was talking sound political sense when he said, "There is no king where the will and not the law has dominion"—the rule is as valid for a corporation as for a Norman prince.

IV

The Modern Corporation in International Affairs

Corporate power in international affairs becomes a matter of major concern in the twentieth-century world. The subject can only be sketched here. A library would be needed to deal with international relations of American corporations, and its content would be surprising. Obviously, American enterprises doing business outside the United States necessarily have relations with their peers outside the United States, and with foreign governments which carry on major economic functions. No management can avoid them; no prudent management could fail to have the equivalent of a diplomatic staff.

The thesis here presented is that in mid-twentieth century these relations, as they have been carried on, are on the whole constructive. Further, they offer a solidly available line of approach toward that degree of world economic co-operation which appears to be essential in the interests both of the United States and of other western-world countries.

The part played by commercial corporations in international affairs has been a favorite target for every sort of comment. Communist propagandists and commentators refer to these relations as an "apparatus of western imperialism," though the fact appears to be that they are infinitely less so than any Soviet trade commissariat or Nazi state-directed corporation. American commentators, often with reason, have been troubled by the dangers inherent in the relations of large corporations to foreign countries, and it is true that there have been plenty of trouble spots. Yet the fact appears to be that the dangers inherent in corporate international relations are much the same as those inherent in any kind of international contact. Attacks are frequently based on the analogies of history: the conduct of affairs by the British East India Company, or by American concessionary companies in the Caribbean has been transposed from the eighteenth and the nineteenth centuries into the twentieth, and has been superimposed as a sort of stereotype picture. This would be about as factual as analyzing twentieth-century democracy on the basis of labor conditions tolerated and accepted by Great Britain or the United States in 1835.

But if many attacks have been meretricious, defense

has been almost equally inept. Most corporations shroud their international arrangements in deepest secrecy. Some try to suggest either that they have none, or that they are of little importance. Most of the information we do possess has been the result of some conflict leading to investigation and sworn testimony, in which a corporate manager appears as a reluctant witness while facts are ferreted out if (and to the extent that) some investigating officer knows enough to ask the right questions. Sometime there will arise (as has been the case in one or two instances) a group of corporate representatives who understand that they do represent quasi-political institutions; that international relations of some kind are essential for the lives of their companies; that then, if properly run, they are beneficial. These men will present the case for or against any particular set of relationships exactly as do well-trained government foreign affairs men explaining the measures taken by their governments, and the reasons for them.

2

The case for the large American corporations in foreign affairs is substantial. They enter foreign affairs because they must. They conduct their relationships at least as successfully as do governments. They have made and can make dangerous mistakes. They also offer a possible avenue of greater adjustment in twentieth-century problems.

The United States is not a socialist country nor likely to become one in the foreseeable future. Its method of operation in the industrial field is predominantly through corporations. Industry by industry, as we have seen, the pattern of a "concentrate" of two, three, or four large corporations controlling more than half the industry has steadily established itself. Though in general the base of American industry is the American market, great areas of that industry powerfully affect or depend upon foreign markets, sometimes as sellers, ofttimes as buyers of raw material. The aggregate of these impacts makes the state of American business the greatest single economic factor in the foreign affairs of the free world.

But America herself is equally in the grip of this complex of forces. The state of our industry and the continuity of its growth directly turns on scientific progress. Now the United States has no monopoly on scientific research or technical brains. Scientists unanimously agree that technical progress turns on an endless process of cross-fertilization and constant world-wide exchange of ideas and knowledge. Technically as well as economically, the United States, for all its huge area and huge market, is merely a vast nexus through and from which economic and scientific lines radiate in all directions. Inevitably many American corporations, especially those in the greatest basic lines of production, affect, and are affected by, policies and regulations enforced in like fields of economic activity elsewhere in the world. The growing size, diversity, and complication of American economic operation suggest that impacts of this kind will increase rather than decrease. A program of isolationism or pure nationalism is sheer impossibility when applied to the mid-twentieth-century industrial and economic life of this country.

American industry, in this context, has really only three alternatives from which to choose.

It could ask the United States government to conquer so much of overseas territory as it may determine to be necessary or desirable. This would follow straight eighteenth-century lines, under which the political state was induced to undertake conquest of foreign areas or territories by diplomacy or arms, or to set up dominated areas within which industry would get what it wished— in other words, economic imperialism, European-style, as practiced a century and a half ago. This is considered immoral and uncivilized by the non-Communist world of the twentieth century; and it has proved increasingly impractical as the nineteenth-century imperial system broke up under impact of local nationalism.

Second, American industry can, without asking government intervention, seek to buy foreign materials and sell products abroad on a straight competitive basis. Something can be done, and always is being done along this line; the twentieth-century world has allowed a certain scope for international competition. But the limits are close and narrow. At present most countries (the United States included) refuse to permit much competition from foreign sellers within their borders where they are able to supply the desired goods or services with home talent and organization. Most countries allow and foster competition in purchasing these products. Yet even in that field, countries supplying raw materials to foreign companies are steadily demanding, with increasing force, that the raw materials they sell shall be manufactured, as well as mined, extracted or grown within their borders. Venezuela, for example, is quite prepared to sell crude oil to foreign companies; but she increasingly insists that, to the fullest extent possible, refining shall be done in Venezuela. Some countries, such as India, go to extreme lengths in this policy. We pay lip-service to open markets and free competition, but realistically in international commerce it must be recognized that competition is no wide-open door. The nineteenth-century Britannic world of Cobden and Bright has refused to come back.

The third alternative open to corporate managements is co-operation of some kind. Practically, this is what usually happens.

The United States has chosen to regard co-operative agreements in foreign trade as violating the American antitrust laws and is bringing action now to dissolve the world-wide marketing agreements alleged to exist between the great oil companies. Few, if any, foreign nations see any sense in our attitude. To most European countries, the doctrine of unrestricted and unregulated international competition is regarded as sheer irresponsibility. To them a cartel of companies, allocating markets, regulating production more or less in accordance with presumed demand, and so forth, is the normal and intelligent way of dealing with a situation; unless, of course, the governments make the necessary arrangements by straight treaty. Some European businessmen concede that in a market as large as the United States, or perhaps the Soviet Union or China, unrestricted competition may be a successful means of handling national economic problems. But they point out that even in large countries of less size—for example, Great Britain, Germany, or France—the national market, however substantial, is too small to permit this in most industries. Some say forthrightly that unless nations themselves are able to work together in a sort of planned economy—which they are frequently not able to do—best let the producing units themselves do the planning.

The international cartels in Europe to which not infrequently American concerns were parties (and indeed had to be if they were to operate in Europe on any substantial scale) were in reality crude industrial planning instruments without which European industrial life would have been anarchic chaos.

The cartel pattern on the other side of the Atlantic is thus considered not a vice, but a useful method of international arrangement. In the closing months of 1944, the writer presided over the International Civil Aviation Conference held in Chicago to set up arrangements by which international air traffic could be undertaken as soon as warfare had stopped. It seemed perfectly natural for Lord Swinton, representing the British delegation, to suggest that the British and American interests split trans-Atlantic traffic between them, and that the United States have jurisdiction to determine what Western Hemisphere nations should participate, while Britain in consultation with her associates determined the distribution of air traffic on the continent of Europe and the Near East. The conflict between the American and the British conception was obviously complete. But to an Englishman it was as normal to cartelize and divide up the market as it was to most of the American civil aviation industry to insist on free competition in an open sky.

Many Europeans do agree with American strictures on the actual work of cartels. They admit freely that the cartel industrial planning has often been short-sighted, sometimes unintelligent, and frequently down-right oppressive. But they lay this not to the existence of the cartel institution which they are not ready to scrap, but to default or failure of the cartel managers to do a good job. The criterion is whether the cartel turns out a good economic and social result. Even the European critics see no more point in discarding the cartel because it can do a bad piece of work than an American would see point in abolishing American state legislatures because they can and sometimes do pass unwise or oppressive legislation.

Enlightened foreign students of the subject, for example Paul van Zeeland of Belgium, sometimes make an even more telling point. The history of international governmental co-operation in the economic field has been grim and disappointing. Political states and their governments have had a fabulously difficult time in working together on anything, and particularly so in working together on common economic problems. Whatever the reason, this is the historical fact. The companion fact is that great economic organizations have found it and do find it possible to work together. Actually, where political states do not interfere, they co-operate more often than not. Longer-headed European statesmen have found in this a ray of hope in a difficult international world. Here at least are national institutions which seem to be able to find common ground, to discuss, to compromise, to agree and adjust rather than fight. Far from being a danger to be eradicated, this appeals to some as a method to be encouraged and guided. Out of this line of thinking came the idea of a brilliant Frenchman, Jean Monnet. He proposed a legally sovereign system of internationally directed cartels over coal and iron in Western Europe, having free commercial passage across certain national borders. This has now emerged, via the "Schumann Plan," as the "European Coal and Steel Community," a semi-sovereign supranational body, capable of planning the West European coal and steel production and distributing it unobstructed by nationalist barriers in certain countries. To this community the United States government has recently accredited an Ambassador.

None of this was accepted doctrine at the close of World War II. Most Americans interested in the subject and some Europeans considered that the integration and cartelization of European industrial concerns was inherently evil—though a vast diversity of grounds were stated. Some thought that the German industrial concerns—many of which had co-operated powerfully with the Nazi government—were primarily responsible for the Nazi movement. In that idea, I think it is clear now that Russian propaganda played some part; breaking up the old cartels tended to undermine the industrial structure of Western Europe, making conquest by Communism easier. Under cover of the operation, also, a lively bit of class warfare could be carried on. Others, untouched by Communist ideas, based their antagonisms principally on the ground that the European cartels had done a bad job, creating multimillionaires on the one hand, and on the other depressing the living standards of labor, while raising price levels at the expense of the consuming public. In their favor was the sharp contrast between the rapidly increasing material standard of living in the United States extending to all classes, and the static position of labor, peasants, and less fortunate strata in European society; and the legalized concentrates and monopolies organized into national and international cartels under European custom and law were held responsible.

Some truth could be found in all these contentions; but few in the United States squarely faced the problem as it presented itself abroad. The fact appeared to be that modern industrial production had outgrown the breeches of all the relatively small European nation-states. The electric bulb and lamp industry, largely developed by the Phillips companies and organized from The Netherlands and roughly paralleling the work done by General Electric here, could obtain cheap production only by producing a volume of output sufficient to pave every street in The Netherlands with electric light bulbs; and to do that, it had to draw materials from two or three continents. Illustrations could be multiplied. If European industry was to proceed on a modern industrial basis, the corporation or enterprise conducting it had to enter other countries both to sell and to buy; had to make terms with the industry of other countries to avoid being strangled by tariff or quota restrictions; had to equate purchases and sales so that at least a modicum of balance would exist in foreign exchange. In practice, the corporations engaged in these industries combined. The cartel system in Europe was essentially an industrial planning system—with the advantages and the dangers inherent in any planning system.

Europeans facing the problem of decartelization assumed, as did the British Labor Party, that the real alternative was not competition but socialism. Under a socialist system the planning function is performed by the state, equipped with substantially complete power since the socialist state actually does the work of production and distribution. In that case, of course, international planning could be done entirely by political governments and cartel agreements would be replaced by international treaties. Assuming the socialist premise, this was honest and solid thinking—as far as it went. But it encountered one major and insuperable obstacle. Political states have the greatest difficulty in making agreements covering economics. A major effort is needed to secure agreement of any group of governments in respect to handling of production, distribution, and international trade, and socialist governments seem no more willing to agree than capitalist governments. In contrast, a major effort is needed to prevent any group of corporations from reaching some sort of market understanding, as the long history of the Sherman law in the United States amply attests. Given the present system of sovereign national states of relatively small area and population (the present case of Europe), unplanned economy meant abandoning many of the possibilities of the modern industrial system. Planning meant either accepting the cartel instrumentality, or seeking an untried and relatively unsuccessful statist system under improbable international agreement. The

European knew quite well that, economically, the Austrian Empire had been far more successful than the group of states emerging from it after World War I; and, for that matter, the Napoleonic Empire had been economically more successful than the unrelated European principalities overthrown by the French armies. But the empires had gone, and few, it seemed, wanted them back.

European thinkers accordingly saw the question somewhat as we are posing it here: a problem of power. Locking all the power in a single, world-directed empire, was quite satisfactory to a Russian Communist or to a Nazi statist—always providing that the power came to rest in his particular party or group. The socialist came to somewhat the same conclusion though he was prepared to allow a much higher degree of self-determination to individuals within the system of planning as he conceived it. Hardly anyone cared to assume the risk, in twentieth-century Europe as it actually exists, of unplanned industry: the danger was too great that political forces engendered would create conditions under which industry would sharply contract, and some of it might disappear. This meant risking unemployed workers, failure of supply of consumer goods, deterioration of the standard of living, possible political disorder, in brief, a step backward in civilization—the kind of backward step in fact that no American politician would risk for a moment if he were faced with similar choice. Unless therefore the European could somehow eliminate all barriers inherent in national boundaries, securing a single market, including many countries, he was unwilling to take the risk.

On closer examination one tends to agree with him. The farce-tragic element in the entire picture lies, of course, in the position of the Soviet Union. There, the relatively large market for industrial mass production did exist; the American system of large-scale units with a degree of competition was admirably adapted to the vast population and space of the Soviet Empire. There is considerable statistical basis for believing that the condition of the Russian masses and the strength of the Soviet state would have progressed far more rapidly under the American system than it has under Communist rule—though historical might-have-beens never can be demonstrated. In historical fact, the Communist movement was precisely a movement dedicated not only to planning but to a particular detailed and specific kind of planning with the state as dictatorial planner. As the issue developed in Europe, the line was drawn not between unplanned economy and planned economy but between the methods of planning, the objectives sought to be achieved, and the great contest turned on location of the planning power. In non-statist Western Europe effective planning power was factually located in the business, industrial and banking groups rather than in the state, though their planning operations are permitted and commonly assisted by their national governments. In the main, the planning power is still held by that group.

With this stubborn fact, American corporations carrying on overseas operations must deal.

In certain parts of the world an American corporation must do its business frankly and openly with the foreign government, with or without assistance from the United States Department of State. American oil companies doing business in Venezuela, American copper companies doing business in Chile, American sugar companies doing business in the Dominican Republic, for example, deal directly with the competent authorities of these states. Though corporate practice is far from uniform, it would seem that most American corporations prefer to deal direct rather than through American Embassies or diplomatic officials, though the diplomats can be of help under some circumstances. Some of the larger corporations have continuous and careful reports made to them on the attitudes and aptitudes of the American diplomatic officials, rating them according to their probable usefulness in advancing or protecting the company's interest.

The interests of an American corporation doing business abroad at any time do not necessarily coincide with the then current policy of the United States government. The corporate management in such case has to decide whether to try to conform the policy of the company to that of the government, or whether to oppose the policy of Washington and carry on operations contrary to it abroad to the extent they consider safe. This situation arises in a number of contexts.

Whenever the United States endeavors to restrict the flow of goods, such divergences almost invariably arise. In the years 1940-1941, it became evident that the National-Socialist government of Germany was using German trade operations to organize anti-American fifth columns in many parts of South America. A number of German mercantile houses in South American cities were acting as sales and service agents for certain powerful American corporations. Some of them had been brought within the scope of the Nazi organization. To break up the German fifth-column organization, the government of the United States requested American concerns to withdraw their agencies from houses known to be working under the orders of the Hitler government. This was both inconvenient and financially disadvantageous for the American concerns. Most of them promptly followed the request from our Department of State. One famous corporation objected, and its vice-president was sent to Washington to argue with the Under-Secretary of State. His argument was direct and simple. His corporation, he said, was not in politics of any kind. If the United States government wished to have a quarrel with the Nazi government of Germany, that was the government's privilege; but his corporation in its foreign operations could not be involved, and did not feel bound to accommodate itself to American policy expressed in a "moral embargo." The corporation subsequently changed its position and accepted the American policy, whether as a result of changed opinion, or of shrewd appreciation of the fact that the government of the United States felt strongly enough about it to exert pressure. Ordinarily the divergence is not as clean-cut. In a somewhat similar situation involving moral embargo, another great corporation argued that it had contracts outstanding and that unless it filled them, it might be liable for damage. It wanted to be guaranteed against any financial damage. Against these must be set a far greater number of other cases where no less famous American corporations looked over the situation, discussed American policy with the competent officials in the Department of State, and decided to accept risks and even clear losses in aid of American policy.

Less dramatic, but rather more puzzling, are situations in which a powerful American corporation has interests in a foreign country and the government of that country engages in policies adverse to these interests. The American Department of State in all normal situations endeavors to support the interests of its nationals, including its corporations, abroad. But occasions arise in which the government considers that the corporation ought to make concessions to the foreign government in the interest of sound economics, or perhaps of continued friendly relations between the two nations. Not infrequently this occurs when the corporation has secured, and operates under, concessions or contracts with a foreign government, perhaps negotiated many years ago, which have become oppressive or which appear with some justification to be violative of the sovereign status of the country. The interest of the United States is to obtain a just and equitable solution; this probably also is the long-run interest of the corporation. But the short-run corporation interest is to maintain its position to the limit. The corporation is in background a private business enterprise, and by habit considers that a contract is a contract. But in foreign relations, contracts of this kind are more nearly like treaties; and treaties have to be handled with a wide degree of flexibility, else the system breaks down. Occasionally the result is a three-cornered negotiation between the corporation officials and the government involved, with American diplomatic officials sitting in as mediators. The famous "50-50" arrangement settling the outstanding dispute between the American oil companies doing business there and the government of Venezuela is a good illustration, though the turning point in that negotiation probably was a realization on the part of the oil companies, brought about by Mr. Nelson Rockefeller, that a fairer division of profit between them and the government was essential from all points of view.

Some companies with large and widespread overseas interests frequently maintain their own edition of a tiny State Department. Their overseas subsidiaries, branches, and representatives report more or less regularly. Their economic departments keep them informed of business and financial conditions. They have their own resident or traveling diplomats. Emphasis is given to cultivating personal relations with the proper officials in government both in America and abroad and, so far as possible, in developing a favorable state of public relations. The ablest and most skillful managements endeavor to remain apart from foreign partisan or factional political struggles. This is contrary to the popular impression in the United States—an impression largely derived from the history of the nineteenth century. (It is true that from 1840 to 1900 large American enterprises frequently sought to obtain, and occasionally achieved, control of governments of some of the weaker countries by financing political parties, bribing officials and occasionally supporting outright revolution. A century ago, in the case of the great filibuster, William Walker, who twice succeeded in subverting the government of Nicaragua, American business supplied a good deal of the money—as, for that matter, other American interests supplied the money which led to Walker's eventual overthrow and death. But that was in 1854.) For the past thirty years every American corporation has known that political involvement of this kind was commonly unprofitable, necessarily dangerous and in the long run suicidal.

More often the facts run squarely counter to popular impression. American corporations working abroad are frequently under pressure from political groups within the country to align themselves with one or another of them. At its simplest this takes the form of solicitation for contributions to campaign funds or party treasuries; sometimes, more active participation is sought. Fear is created that failure to aid or contribute may produce

136

adverse measures should the soliciting party come into power, or conversely, hope of favors is held out. In at least one well-known instance, an American Ambassador to Cuba, Mr. Spruille Braden, moved to insulate American corporations from such pressure by announc· ing publicly that American policy opposed participa tion by American enterprise in Cuban politics and that the American Embassy specifically requested that no American concern make contributions to any political campaign fund.

Occasionally, however, the situation works out differ- ently, and American corporations are formally called in to assist in effecting international arrangements with the assent, or perhaps at the instance, of the govern- ments involved. After the government of Premier Mossadegh had caused Iran to seize the installations of the Anglo-Iranian Oil Company, a British conces- sionary corporation, the crisis stood at stalemate for some time. Adjustment was finally reached permitting reopening of the Anglo-Iranian refinery. But by that time the market for Iranian oil had been absorbed by other suppliers, largely American. Solution of the crisis required not only putting the Anglo-Iranian plant back into operation but marketing its product. A group of eight oil companies, five of them American and three European, was got together. It was announced on April

12, 1954, that each of these companies had agreed to market specific percentages of the Iranian oil, thereby restoring to Iran the outlet for its product which it had lost through Mossadegh's ill-advised attempt at expropriation. Though the record is not yet available, this was unquestionably done at the request of the governments of Great Britain and the United States, in which presumably the government of Iran joined. The result was to settle an internal political issue, a difficult international crisis, and an economic problem for both Iran and Great Britain. Corporate operations in foreign countries have created plenty of problems. It is fair to note that they have also solved some, and probably if full balance were struck, have resolved more than they have created.

Nonetheless, corporate policy does affect the internal politics of other countries by sheer force of economic circumstances and this is unavoidable. The corporate operations, for one thing, directly affect the amount of foreign exchange brought into or taken from a foreign country; if the country is small, this will materially affect the position of its own currency. For another, the expansion of a corporation's activity may be a material factor in the level of employment, its wage policies materially affect the wage level, the taxes it pays are frequently a major item in the country's revenue and fiscal position. These in turn may very well depend on the price policies adopted by the corporation. In a word, the corporation must consider the effect its purely commercial policies have on the country involved. An adverse effect tends to weaken the government in power and strengthen the opposition; a beneficial effect tends to strengthen the government in power and to weaken the opposition. The most conscious and responsible corporate management cannot insulate its operations from these factors which necessarily have political results. The twentieth-century world has built up and apparently demands commercial and economic relations far outrunning the historical boundaries of nationalist countries; but nationalism still is the basis of international life and corporations are fated to struggle with this unrelated dichotomy. Internationally, as well as nationally, large corporations have found themselves strong and sometimes determinative factors in an unsolved economic power-complex, and must feel their way. Perhaps the twenty-first century will see a world in which nationalism is fitted into great regional federations in which interests are pooled for the purpose of economic policy as is the case between the states of the United States. But we have not got there yet.

It can be said that relations carried on by private corporations directly with foreign governments, when handled by enlightened men, with broad human sympathies, and with respect for the countries in which their companies operate, and for the people with which they deal, are at least as satisfactory as the economic relations worked out by government-to-government negotiation. Frequently the weakness in their conduct lies in the fact that corporations do not normally develop men trained to consider all the aspects of foreign relations. A promoted Vice-President in Charge of Production or Director of Sales has not been trained for this sort of thing. More recently, corporate managements, appreciating this fact, have been drawing into their staffs some of the abler men trained in the Foreign Service of the American State Department, as the United States Steel Company recently did when it took Mr. Walter Donnelly, a distinguished Foreign Service officer, and made him their "diplomatic" representative in South America, and as the Electric Bond and Share Company did some years ago when it engaged former Ambassador George Messersmith to represent its interests in Mexico. The Standard Oil Company of New Jersey has built up a very competent staff of men to handle its relations in the Near East and the General Motors Company has sought to give special training in foreign affairs to the men assigned to represent it overseas.

The system has had its success, and its failures. Its weakness is that corporate representatives, in terms, represent a money-making, profit-making enterprise. The fact does not altogether correspond to the hypothesis. Economic relations which in turn affect political relations have a broader base than that of a mere income statement. Corporate representatives working in foreign countries increasingly understand that, and so do the corporate managements themselves. The unresolved problem is at least as much a problem of the organization of international political relations as of divergence of interests between the business corporation and the foreign country in which it works—or, for that matter, between the corporation and the interests of its own country. When carried on by enlightened men with respect for the countries in which they work, and with enlightened policy, the results are at least as satisfactory as are economic relations worked out between governments themselves.

Foreign relations of large corporations have been under constant and steady attack from many quarters. Inherently, Americans have distrusted the intrusion of private concerns in foreign affairs, though as has appeared the intrusion is an almost necessary consequence of any overseas operation in size. On the basis of the total available record one can cite many instances of corporate failure in international affairs; not a few of impropriety, and some of clear injustice. Against these must be set a greater and solid mass of substantial economic achievement, resulting in enhanced economic well-being both for the company involved and for the country in which it operates. Any chronicle of twentieth-century foreign relations is chiefly a grim record of tragedy, occasionally relieved by happy highlights of real success. Yet if the entire field of corporate relations with foreign governments is reviewed for the period, say, from 1930 to 1950, the conclusion may be hazarded that the results of corporations' conduct of foreign affairs in their chosen area compares favorably with the results of the conduct of foreign affairs by governments.

Foreign relations so carried on, however, are subject to one major reservation. The management of an American corporation in conducting them is using its power absolutely. There is no effective review. In extreme circumstances, of course, the political machinery of the United States may be invoked or may intrude. The Congress may pass legislation limiting the corporate power, or, more often, outlawing particular operations. The influence of the executive branch of the government may be brought to bear for or against some particular corporate policy. But this occurs only when matters have reached a stage of conflict, or irritation, or, less often, when the policy of the corporation is at odds with the policy of the United States. Then, an impact occurs between the corporation and the community represented by the United States, and the matter is worked out in conflict or in accord as the case may be.

Such clashes occur rarely. The weakness of the situation lies in the fact that the government of the United States must then attempt to resolve a situation it did not create, and which in the light of hindsight, it commonly insists could have been avoided. Americans have wondered whether the state of their foreign relations really should be left in the hands of private interests—and there is force in the point. In answer it can only be urged that the system, taken by and large, has not worked too badly.

In foreign affairs as in domestic economy, the United States relies on the large corporation as a substantial factor. In foreign as in domestic matters, the American state leaves primary responsibility in the hands of the corporate managers. In foreign as in domestic matters, when the result is conflict with some interest that the community regards as important, the American government steps in and plays a substantial, if not decisive part, in achieving or compelling a solution. Short of such conflict, the modern corporation pursues its own policy.

In sum, a large American corporation with overseas interests operates through a set of relationships and agreements maintained and arrived at either by direct contact with other governments or by direct contact with other large corporations. By co-ordinating policy, the large American corporation finds and maintains its place in an international system permitting it to operate. This is, substantially, the method by which production, and distribution, in the Western world is carried on.

3

Large corporations, like nations, have encountered the danger of world anarchy, have sought safety in balance of power, and from time to time have attempted in their field experiments in world government. To this last point, attention may be directed. In point of surprising fact, the large American corporations in certain fields have more nearly achieved a stable and working world government than has yet been achieved by any other institution.

The outstanding illustration is the case of the oil industry. The facts here given are chiefly derived from a report from the Federal Trade Commission, and in part from the allegations by the Department of Justice in a current civil action against the Socony Oil Company and a group of other foreign and domestic petroleum concerns. Full statement of the position of the oil companies has not yet been made, and presumably will not be complete until the case is tried, if it ever is. The government's statement tends to be unfavorable to the companies' point of view, and certainly is not accepted by the companies. Antitrust legalistics aside (world affairs being what they are), the story is amazing, and far from being any picture of crime.

The story, in salient outline, is substantially this.

In the year 1926 a relative balance of power existed in the world's oil markets. It had been reached by a complex series of bilateral and multilateral agreements between the world's large oil companies in respect of various oil fields. Geographically these extended all the way from the Dutch East Indies and Iran to Venezuela and Bolivia. Seven companies had an overwhelming majority of world production: Royal Dutch Shell, Anglo-Persian, Standard Oil of New Jersey, Socony-Vacuum, Gulf, Texas, Atlantic Refining Company. The balance was uneasy. The history behind its attainment had been tangled and dramatic. Governments supporting one or another interest had at times been brought to the point of conflict. Local agreements, division of territory, and cross-purchases of stock in development companies and so on, had temporarily resolved these situations. They were in dubious equilibrium in 1926 when a commercial conflict broke out in India.

There, Socony-Vacuum Oil Company had purchased Russian oil from wells previously belonging to Royal Dutch Shell, but later nationalized by the Soviet government. Shell, belonging to British and Dutch interests, resented this; in any event, a price war broke out between Socony and Shell in the Indian market. Shell presently extended the war to the United States, directly invading the American market. (This is why, in 1954, gasoline stations selling Shell oil are found in many parts of the United States.) Socony promptly counterattacked by entering the British market, and competition and a price war thus became general.

At this point the more responsible brains in the oil industry went to work on the situation, with the result that in September 1928, a conference was held at Achnacarry Castle in Britain, the home of Sir Henry Deterding, head of Shell. It is reported that the heads of Standard Oil of New Jersey, Shell, and Anglo-Persian oil companies were the negotiators. The result was a document entitled, "Pool Association," but later referred to as the "Achnacarry Agreement," or by the more descriptive name of the "As Is" Agreement. It was, in effect, a treaty of commercial peace concluding an economic war between great corporations. As the war had become world-wide, the peace necessarily had to deal with world conditions in the oil industry. It established what may be described, without too much exaggeration, as the most successful experiment in economic world government thus far achieved in the twentieth century.

Summarized, the "As Is" Agreement adopted seven governing principles.

(1) Each company was to retain the percentage of the market, everywhere, enjoyed at the time by that company. (Diplomats would call this "peace on the basis of the *status quo*.")

(2) The existing facilities of all companies were to be made available to competitors at not less than actual cost but at a cost less than any company would incur if it built new facilities.

(3) New facilities were to be built only to supply increased consumption requirements.

(4) Each producing area was to have the advantage arising from its geographical position—that is, should sell in the nearest market.

(5) Supplies for each market should be drawn from the nearest producing area.

(6) Surplus production in any producing area was not to be "dumped" in other areas to the disturbance

of the price structure there prevailing. In practice this meant that surplus production could be sold anywhere at the prevailing price—but if it could not be sold at that price must be shut in.

(7) No measures were to be taken which would materially increase the cost of producing oil.

The domestic market and import trade of the United States was excepted from this arrangement, lest the companies agreeing to it find themselves in conflict with the Sherman antitrust law; but apparently the American companies hoped to use the Webb-Pomerene Act and the conservation principles which later emerged in American domestic legislation so as to give substantial effect to the "As Is" principles.

This was in the nature of a treaty expressing the policy. Implementation of the policy required further working out. Thus, quotas were agreed to, each company's quota being an amount equal to the percentage of the market it had had in the year 1928. If the market increased, the quota increased in volume, though not in percentage. For the purposes of transport, each company agreed to pool the tankers and ships which it was not using. The group assigned these ships at prevailing rates to other members of the pool who desired them. Supplies of oil were routed from the nearest producing point in the control of any group member to the nearest market. In practice this meant that a company could always purchase from the producer nearest its market the petroleum needed to satisfy its demand; a price scale was agreed on, based on the price prevailing at United States Gulf ports. Wherever the oil was produced, and wherever sold, a freight charge was added equal to the freight which would have been payable if the oil had been brought from a United States Gulf port.

An association of the companies was formed, with an administrative body made up of one representative of each member. This was authorized to set up a statistical unit, and a management unit, which should inform members of total demand in all areas, allocate quotas and direct shipments, administer the pooled transport facilities, prepare freight-rate charges, post basing prices, and act as a clearing house for sales between members of the association. But the administrative unit apparently never was brought into being. It was found practicable to cover the ground by individual company arrangements, and the Achnacarry Agreement appears really to have been used as a controlling basis of company policy determination, made effective through a series of regional agreements. Even in the oil industry, world government found it advisable to split the problem into manageable areas rather than to attempt to handle the entire planet as a unit.

So, on January 20, 1930, the same three companies negotiated the so-called "Memorandum for European Markets" as an implementation of the principles of the Achnacarry Agreement. A method of enforcing quota agreements was worked out; an "over-trader" who had sold more than his quota at the expense of the other members was required to adjust with an "under-trader" (a company which had lost part of its quota market) preferably by transferring customers to the under-trader or, if this was impractical, by paying to the under-trader the profit on the products the over-trader had sold beyond his quota. There were also fines and penalties for persistent over-trading, though the writer knows of no case where these were imposed. Local agreements for price-fixing (entirely legal in Europe) provided a method by which the association members could decide; each member had one vote for each 1 per cent of the market reserved to it by its quota. Outsiders could be admitted to the group by unanimous consent, but not under conditions more favorable than those granted to original members. Local committees, required to meet every two weeks and exchange statistics between themselves and outsiders, were to establish quotas year by year. They fixed terms and prices of sale, adjusted and exchanged quotas by intragroup agreement, determined penalties, and generally were supposed to co-operate in maintaining and extending the group position. Members were prohibited from acquiring secret interests in oil-producing concerns except by consent of the Big Three.

Underneath the "Memorandum for European Markets," local agreements presently were found necessary. Such subsidiary agreements in time were drawn for Britain, Germany, Austria, Switzerland, Poland, Spain, and Rumania. Attempt was made to negotiate for Soviet participation, but this apparently failed.

In 1932, there were two "As Is" committees in operation, one in London and one in New York. The supply arrangements for the world scheme were generally administered from New York; the quota and price arrangements (operative outside the United States) were reportedly administered in London. The London "As Is" committee, reportedly comprising representatives of Standard Oil Company of New Jersey, Anglo-Persian Company, Royal Dutch Shell, Socony-Vacuum, Gulf, Texas, Atlantic (and possibly Sinclair), recodified the "Memorandum for European Markets" with some modifications, including liberalization of the terms on which outsiders might be admitted. Arrangements were made for dividing new or "virgin" market territories into five zones, with provisions for a quota for each zone, among the participants. There were difficulties. American economy was already in depression, and with it came overproduction of petroleum in the Gulf ports. The resulting fall of prices in the United States threw out of balance some of the price arrangements, and notably that established with one "outside" group—the Rumanian oil producers; the difficulty was not resolved until in 1933 the National Recovery Act was put into effect in the United States and an N.R.A. Oil Industry Code established minimum prices in the United States Gulf area. Yet, on the whole, the Achnacarry arrangement is credited with stabilizing the oil industry during the violent economic disturbances of 1933-1934.

The Agreement appears to have been redrafted in the spring or early summer of 1934, the redrafted document being known as the "Draft Memorandum of Principles." This revised the quota system. It made certain European price-fixing arrangements rather more flexible. Of interest is the fact that it provided (among other things) for reduction of unnecessary advertising costs, road signs, billboards, and the like. Under it, subordinate marketing agreements and groups were set up in Sweden, Great Britain, France, Germany, Rumania, Belgium and The Netherlands, Denmark, Norway, Finland, Argentina, Chile, Brazil, Mexico, Cuba, the Lesser Antilles, and in the area east of Suez. Production and supply agreements were made governing most

of the South American, the Middle Eastern, and the
Rumanian oil. A number of countries, including Great
Britain, France, and Argentina whose policy is to assist
and administer cartels, aided and encouraged these
agreements, and some contention is made that these
countries actively pressed for the Agreement. The revised arrangements set up under the "Draft Memorandum of Principles" lasted for some years. Standard Oil
Company of New Jersey insists that they were aban-
doned in 1938 and that all activities under it ceased
by 1939. In that year, of course, World War II broke
out, and the oil supply of the world came rapidly under
direct government war controls. The New Jersey company has steadily insisted, and in its Annual Report for
the year 1953 states categorically that it is not a member of any cartel, and doubts whether any cartel exists.
Local cartel arrangements in individual countries sanc-
tioning such agreements, of course, do exist; it is im-
practicable at this time (1954) to draw any conclusions as
to the extent to which the principles of the Achnacarry
Agreement or its successor agreements now survive.

Evaluation of this really remarkable and pragmati-
cally successful experiment in planned economy is difficult to make. The attitudes of different people are
completely opposed. To the European mentality, perhaps especially to the British, arrangements of this sort

represent ordinary common sense: by their criteria, the result was brilliant. To American doctrine at the very least they represent danger, and very possibly criminal restraint of trade. The Federal Trade Commission report detailing the facts was in fact brought out in the summer of 1952 by the Senate Sub-Committee on Small Business, in a context indicating that it was a calculated attack on the oil companies.

The Department of Justice presently indicated that it would bring action against them under the Sherman Antitrust Act. The departmental investigation was pushed to the point of a proposed criminal action and the government lawyers sought to secure by subpoena the testimony of some of the oil companies' personnel, together with records and files. The Department of Justice among other things attempted to subpoena the records of Anglo-Iranian Oil Company. At this point the British government promptly objected on the ground that this was a British company, and that British records were not subject to the jurisdiction of American courts. The dispute became heated. The National Security Council took cognizance of the matter. It was later reported that, pursuant to its recommendation made on January 11, 1953, the then Attorney General, James P. McGranery, opened negotiations for compromise. He was reported to have offered to drop the proposed criminal antitrust action if the international oil companies would agree not to move to dismiss a civil antitrust action and comply with a subpoena permitting examination of their files—a proposal summarily rejected by the companies. Though the possibility of American antitrust action is by no means ended, there is at present an apparent absence of interest in pushing it. In any case, it is reasonably clear that no American action can effectively enforce the Sherman Antitrust Act principles throughout the entire world.

The fact was that from 1928 to 1929, the period in which the Achnacarry Agreement and its successor arrangements governed the petroleum supply of the world, there was peace, and there was production, and there was distribution, and there was a stable and reasonably acceptable price. By absolute standards, the agreement has to be accounted a success. Plenty of peace treaties have had a worse fate. Criticism would have to be based on hypothetical comparison between the actual results and those which might have been attained. Obviously the major oil companies did not lose by the Achnacarry arrangements, but then there is little virtue to be found in a losing operation. There is the possibility that the companies' profits were too high, that the prices charged consumers were greater than necessary, and that the group operations tended to discourage local development of crude supply and refining capacity (such development by the great companies went on apace). Probably the only conclusion capable of being drawn is that in any planned economy, national or international, production and stability is gained at the expense of some restriction of freedom of action; the Achnacarry plan certainly reaped the gains, and probably entailed the disadvantages also.

But, if we are indulging "might-have-beens," there is no solid reason to assume that unrestricted world competition would have produced more satisfactory results. After World War I, the mad drive of British, French, and American oil companies into the Persian Gulf area almost provoked warfare. Greater contests with greater irritations and perhaps more catastrophic results might well have taken place as the Arabian and Near Eastern fields increasingly attracted powerful commercial and national interests. Petroleum prices might have been lower in many areas from time to time had unrestricted competition prevailed; but even that is not certain. For in case of competition each company would have had to maintain its own fleet of tankers and transports without full use. It is improbable that oil could have been regularly delivered from the nearest producing field to the nearest consuming market, as the

Achnacarry Agreement provided. More likely, each company would have had to transport oil from its own production fields (wherever located) to such markets as it had. Almost inevitably costs would have been higher, and they would presumably have been eventually reflected in price. Competition, it must be repeated, is one thing when there are an infinite number of small producing and selling units. It is something quite else when a few giants struggle with each other for control of supply, entry into markets, and control of consumer outlet.

As an experiment in world economic government, the corporations cannot on this record be accused of failure.

4

Two observations obtrude themselves at the close of any review, however cursory, of corporations as institutions by which foreign relations are conducted. The first is necessarily a comment on the current international relations themselves. The second is a note as to the position in which corporations of institutional size find themselves as they carry on international commerce as the twentieth-century revolution develops.

The twentieth-century revolution is steadily, ineluctably, breaking up the classic organization of international relations. It is imposing a new organization of affairs whose nature and outlines we can only dimly apprehend. The historic bearer of language, culture, traditions, loyalty, comradeships, has been and still is the sovereign nation-state. But the economic life of the civilized world, and the standard of living demanded by the peoples of twentieth-century nation-states is not being maintained, and apparently cannot be maintained, within the sovereign-state framework. It is possible that the Russian-Chinese imperial complex (itself not a nation but an alliance) may be large enough, and its resources may vary enough, to be self-contained, though this is extremely doubtful. It is certain that no smaller unit can be self-contained for more than the briefest space of historical time. Throughout the entire world the twentieth century has swiftly built and is continuously building new and great cities on a rapidly expanding industrial base. Here is a metropolis like São Paulo in Brazil, in size comparable to Chicago; there, rise smaller but substantial cities on the Atlantic and Mediterranean coasts in Africa, South America, and Asia; from Pasadena to Ceylon, from Capetown to the Ural Mountains. Maintenance of these cities, and of the populations which rightly or wrongly are thronging to them by millions, depends on a volume and variety of production and commerce which cannot be limited by national frontiers born of past historical accident. The United States itself now finds aluminum a national necessity, and draws its raw material from Guiana and the West Indies, to be manufactured in plants scattered from the banks of the St. Lawrence or the Tennessee rivers to the American Northwest. Some of this aluminum must go at once to South America, if Brazilian, Argentine, and Peruvian cities are to endure. To maintain necessary American production of steel, the Caribbean Basin has been explored for ore and manganese, and as a result the area around Trenton, New Jersey, and hundreds of thousands of Americans dwelling there, is coming to live on huge plants depending for their very existence on fleets of company ships bringing ore from cities built and owned by Bethlehem and United States Steel companies on the Orinoco River in Venezuela to the plants of these same companies on the banks of the Delaware. Illustrations could be multiplied one hundred times without overstating the case. The present political framework of foreign affairs is nationalist. The present economic base is not. The classic nation-state is no longer capable, by itself alone, either to feed and clothe its people, or to defend its borders.

This stubborn fact silently and implacably sits at every council table, and in every Ministry of Foreign Affairs, and by the side of every military Chief of Staff;

and, without uttering a word, enters every discussion. One may applaud the fact, or recoil from it. What cannot be done is to escape from it.

To build the underlying economic foundation of national life in the twentieth-century revolution, great enterprises had to be constructed capable of moving across, beyond and outside national lines. It may be argued, as Professor Eugene Rostow of Yale has done in respect of the petroleum industry, that much smaller-scale enterprises should and could have been relied on, and would have received a better result. The fact was that the great corporate enterprises did achieve the result. No substitute has actually emerged, save possibly the international operations of state commissariats. But state commissariats of the style used by the Nazi government in Germany and by the Communist government in the Soviet Union, have been able to function thus far only within an imperial system—that is, by conquering or subordinating to their political domination the countries outside their own in which they operate, and in form or fact annexing them to a central core of empire. The large commercial corporations on the other hand, whatever their defects, have in the main been able to coexist with governments other than their own, outside their homelands, and to fulfill the economic tasks they have assumed.

Governments themselves meanwhile struggle with the implications of this phase of the twentieth-century revolution, seeking to bring international relations more nearly into line with the stark necessities imposed by economics and by defense. Much of the news which flickers across the daily headlines proceeds out of this struggle. The Soviet Union, silently and relentlessly, builds an empire and expands it. The Western Powers endeavor to forge regional groups like the Organization of American States, first planned at Mexico City in 1945; like the North Atlantic Treaty Organization negotiated in 1947; like the Pacific treaty organization currently proposed by Secretary Dulles. But these would be shadow pictures or worse if there were not, beneath them, the commercial organizations which produce, transport, and distribute in adequate quantities oil, iron, copper, bauxite, fibers, foods, rare metals of all kinds, commercial diamonds, rubber, chemicals, and so forth. The vast and thrilling drama of the mid-twentieth century, with its glory and its sordidness, its splendor and its terror, its hope and its fears, comprising the great and tiny aspirations and the heroic and the homely struggles of more than two billion people, is built on just this.

If the great corporations, American, British, French, German, Japanese, Canadian, Brazilian, South African, have not solved the problems of international life, they can claim at least to have kept abreast of them, and in their own sphere, to have kept rather ahead of them. If the job has not been as well done as could be wished, there is no evidence to assume that without them the job would have been done at all. If corporate managements only now and grudgingly apprehend that they must be statesmen rather than salesmen, at least they can claim that politicians whose very business is statesmanship have been no less slow of apprehension. If they and students of them wonder whether these instruments will be apt and continuing foundation blocks in the rapidly building twentieth-century structure, they can retort that the doubt can be directed with equal force toward other and more venerable institutions. If corporations in international commerce live in their time only from day to day, their answer must be that the world itself now lives from day to day, and they must do the best they can. Until the problems of international life, peace, order, and law and of individual protection and realization within it, have been solved the modern institutional corporation must proceed empirically.

The second observation relates to the modern, institutional corporation itself. It has three great qualities. It can energize organizing ability on a huge scale, capable of opening a mine, building a city, or establishing a transport system within a few months, and of articulating production, transport, and distribution on two or three continents. (The United States Steel Company has recently accomplished just that in Venezuela.) It can collect or tap and apply resources and capital in amounts greater than those available to any except the strongest government. And it can recruit and put to work and maintain in continuous and related effort, technical brains and skills running entire the gamut from purest science to the minutiae of production engineering. And it can use all of these three gifts in considerable extent beyond the limits of national borders.

The modern corporation thus has become an international as well as a national instrument. It is a mighty institution which thus far has not become, and has manifested no great desire to become, an independent political force. In international life it is an experiment in non-national organization, pledged only to discharge certain economic functions. An instrument, in fine, worth study and consideration as the twentieth century pushes its turbulent way toward new norms in the life of peoples.

V

Corporate Capitalism and "The City of God"

The preceding chapters suggest rather than describe the extent of the revolution wrought by twentieth-century capitalism. In the long view of history, it is quite probable that the capitalist revolution will be found to be one branch, and not the least significant, of the revolution which the twentieth century has wrought around the world. In many countries of the old world, its instrument was one or another form of socialist organization. In the United States, the chief instrument has proved to be the modern giant corporation.

Only at the middle point of the century has corporate capitalism begun to be aware of this aspect of its function. In process, the real significance was difficult to apprehend. In retrospect, the currents pushing corporate capitalism into the realm of political organization are reasonably clear. Concentration of economic power occurred, driven by the deepest force of the time. Demand for a high standard of living required mass production and mass distribution. Technological advance made this production possible in many of the goods and services considered most essential to the life of a modern population. But, in the quantity and at the prices desired, it had to be accomplished by mass organization. Factually that organization was achieved by great corporate units.

The resulting phenomenon of production in large units in turn set up a grouping within many industries. These groups, although (or perhaps because) they disposed of great powers in their own organizations, in time were oftener than not compelled to attempt or join in planning operations, often embodied in statutory schemes of regulation or legalized stabilization, in lower or higher order of development. In greater or less degree, the practice of national industrial planning is now familiar throughout great areas of the twentieth-century corporate capitalist system. Participation in it is frequently a function, and in any case an occupational hazard, of the managements of large corporations.

Now planning all or any fragment of an economy has enormous implications. This is why any "planned economy" has been feared in America; why economy planned by the state has usually been bitterly fought; why emergence of planning power immediately raises doubts and wonders in the minds of the constituency affected. Naturally; any plan (if it is not a naked power-grab) must be a plan for something, and affects or limits people. Planning, however limited in scope, means planning for some kind of a community, or at least some aspect of a community, deemed by some group to be desirable. Capacity to plan, united with power to give effect to the plan, is perhaps the highest trust granted to statesmen. Its devolution has forced into the hands of many businessmen a complex of problems far beyond their chosen fields, problems overpassing those of producing oil or electrical supplies, of manufacturing steel or motor cars, as the case may be. It may have been naive public relations for an officer of General Motors, proposed for confirmation as Secretary of Defense in the Cabinet of the United States, to say that what was good for General Motors was good for the country, and what was good for the country was good for General Motors; but he could have adduced an impressive array of statistical fact to back up his statement.

For the fact seems to be that the really great corporation managements have reached a position for the first time in their history in which they must consciously take account of philosophical considerations. They must consider the kind of a community in which they have faith, and which they will serve, and which they intend to help to construct and maintain. In a word, they must consider at least in its more elementary phases the ancient problem of the "good life," and how their operations in the community can be adapted to affording or fostering it. They may endeavor to give their views exact statement, or they may merely proceed on undisclosed premises; but, explicitly or implicitly, the premises are there.

Businessmen charged with commercial enterprise are not accustomed to this sort of thinking. As a rule, they reject the idea that this is part of their function. Most corporation executives are acutely aware of the fact that foresight is extremely difficult. Many believe quite frankly, and not without justification, that community welfare is as likely to be developed soundly by hazard as by plan.

The greatest leaders in the corporate field take a contrary view. They forcefully argue that corporations are always citizens of the community in which they operate, while large ones necessarily play a mighty part in the life of their time. It is not possible for them, these men state, to carry on great corporate businesses apart from the main context of American life. If private business and businessmen do not assume community responsibilities, government must step in and American life will become increasingly statist. In consequence, they have urged that corporations must share the burdens of supporting the non-governmental philanthropic and educational institutions which have played so stately a role in the development of twentieth-century America. Mr. Irving Olds, at the time Chairman of the Board of Directors of U. S. Steel Company, made a brilliant and moving address at Yale University, insisting that corporations must contribute to the general educational facilities of the country, such as universities and graduate schools, and that the duties of big business overpass their traditional power to make gifts to those minor or local charities incident to plant and sales operations. He was forcefully supported by Mr. Frank Abrams, Chairman of the Board of Standard Oil Company of New Jersey. Both corporations gave emphatic proof of assent by voting substantial gifts to liberal arts colleges. Twenty-nine states have already passed statutes authorizing corporations, both presently existing and subsequently organized, to make contributions to philanthropy and education. Constitutional validity of one of these statutes—that of New Jersey—was the subject of a recent test case (*A. P. Smith Manufacturing Company v. Ruth Barlow, et al.*) and was forthrightly upheld by the New Jersey Supreme Court. The Supreme Court of the United States dismissed appeal, holding that no Federal question was involved. For practical purposes, the state has authorized corporations to withhold from their shareholders a portion of their profits, channeling it to schools, colleges, hospitals, research, and other good causes.

Twenty years ago, the writer had a controversy with the late Professor E. Merrick Dodd, of Harvard Law School, the writer holding that corporate powers were powers in trust for shareholders while Professor Dodd argued that these powers were held in trust for the entire community. The argument has been settled (at least for the time being) squarely in favor of Professor Dodd's contention.

2

All this certainly underlines the central philosophical problem. If corporations are to make industrial plans, what are the criteria of these plans? If they are to make gifts to support philanthropy, what kind of philanthropy shall they support? If they are trustees for the community, what kind of community interests do they forward? In narrower range, they are explicitly expected to discharge a more or less specialized function by running their businesses and providing a given set of goods and services for the community and in doing so must provide employment for a great number of people. The goods and services they provide, their manner of marketing, the employment conditions they create, the plants they build, all exert powerful influence on the framework of community life. Corporations must also, one supposes, do something for their stockholders as indeed they do, and usually well, even though stockholders do not hold the center of the corporate stage just now. Provision must also be made, it seems, for continued advance in the art and technique of their chosen field or fields.

In larger aspect, the great corporations frequently join, by their own desire or under community pressure, in constructing, setting up, and operating country-wide and national plans tending to assure the continued stability, health, and serviceability of their industries. These are of many kinds, and the means of achieving them have been diverse; but, in the aggregate, plans of some kind cover the more essential parts of the economic machinery of America.

Large corporations, lying outside the range of any nation-wide industry planning as some do, nevertheless within their own operating sphere, appreciably affect community development. They have power to apportion their capital expenditures, on which often depends continued growth in one or another section of the country. Limitations likewise show signs of appearing: there is increasing sentiment, not yet crystallized in law, that they may not withdraw from a community, leaving it a ghost-town because business factors offer greater profit-making opportunities somewhere else.

In the widest of all scenes—the great stage of world politics and world developments—American corporations have begun to appear as active and significant elements. In this country we have not attempted to build titular political structures on them, as has occurred in Europe where M. Jean Monnet has constructed the European Coal and Steel Community as a quasi-sovereign unit on the base of the powerful European cartels. Yet in the petroleum industry, the American oil corporations have informally joined in bringing about more or less orderly development of one of the world's great physical assets and have repeatedly avowed that their operations were the determining factor in national and international development. Other industries have already made their entrance on the field of international affairs.

Growing consciousness of the power thus achieved and its implications has excited a very considerable discussion in the corporate world. Directors, especially those of the largest and most responsible companies, are acutely aware of the problems thus raised. A division of opinion is reported in these circles. One group believes it necessary to pick up the load and tackle the immense responsibilities foreshadowed as did Mr. Olds

171

and Mr. Abrams. Another group take the view that this is not their affair, that they are not equipped to meet it, and that they should find ways of avoiding so great a burden. After all, a board of directors is chosen primarily for its ability in running a particular business. It cannot properly or effectively enter into a whole series of extraneous problems extending all the way from methods of administering individual justice to community development, community organization and community values. This school of thought believes that teachers, scholars, philosophers, and possibly politicians and governments, have to wrestle with these questions: boards of directors cannot. Both views are expressed with honesty and great sincerity.

Corporations still have, perhaps, some range of choice: they can either take an extended view of their responsibility, or a limited one. Yet the choice is probably less free than would appear. Power has laws of its own. One of them is that when one group having power declines or abdicates it, some other directing group immediately picks it up; and this appears constant throughout history. The choice of corporate managements is not whether so great a power shall cease to exist; they can merely determine whether they will serve as the nuclei of its organization or pass it over to someone else, probably the modern state. The present current of thinking and insistence that private rather than governmental decisions are soundest for the community are clearly forcing the largest corporations toward a greater rather than a lesser acceptance of the responsibility that goes with power.

Men squarely facing this problem, in small or in large application, now find themselves, with some surprise, in the realm of philosophy. They have not, it is true, been assigned the job of sketching an Utopia; they only have to take—indeed, can only take—one step at a time. But they can hardly avoid determining the direction of the steps, and the aggregate of their steps in the second half of the twentieth century must necessarily go far toward determining the framework of the American community of the twenty-first. Some sort of hypothesis, however hazy, as to what that community should be, should do, and should look like, seems implicit in this situation.

Some corporations, knowing this, have sought outside advice—General Motors, for example, retained Mr. Peter Drucker for this purpose and his book, *The Concept of the Corporation,* is one of the fruits of it. Others seek guidance from different sources: a famous New York bank has a section which handles corporate foundations set up to discharge their charitable organizations, while the National Industrial Conference Board, an organization of large corporations, works up studies in business policy which it circulates effectively in the corporate field. Still others rely on contacts of their directors with great figures—university presidents, leaders of thought, and eleemosynary foundations, and are guided by them. Occasionally suggestions are made that corporations interested in discharging their novel obligations ought to have a joint working committee, a sort of expanded Community Chest organization, which could make recommendations—and this would have the effect of concentrating still further the mass impact of these great organizations on the future. At least two great business schools—Harvard and Columbia —have offered programs of background information and thinking in the larger ranges of social organization to selected business executives. All this is matrix work, tending toward a body of sophisticated thinking whose aim, properly analyzed, is a conception of a community making for the good life. It seems that, in diverse ways, we are nibbling at the edges of a vast, dangerous, and fascinating piece of thinking. Despite the absence of clear mandate, in broadest outline we are plotting the course by which the twentieth century in America is expected to produce an evolving economic Utopia, and, apparently, the potential actually exists, bringing that dangerous and thrilling adventure within human reach for the first time in recorded history.

This statement will, of course, be promptly questioned. "What," says almost any corporation executive, "do I have to do with Utopias? If we decide to make a gift to Princeton University or to the United Negro College Fund or to the American College in Beirut in the far-off Mediterranean, how do we find ourselves in competition with Plato and his *Republic,* or St. Augustine and his *City of God,* or Sir Thomas More and his *Utopia,* or Sir Francis Bacon and his *New Atlantis?* We have heard of their writings; some of us have read some of them. But we claim no familiarity with their doctrines and their philosophical premises. We have no sort of ambition to run the world, having plenty of headaches right in our own offices. Why not leave us out of this?" The answer is all too plain. A gift is made to Princeton—a gift to a great and free institution. "Splendid," says one board of directors. "We believe in that. In fact, one of the reasons for doing it is precisely to avoid a state-dominated system of education and thinking." Well, it seems one choice has been made. In the coming "City of God' the state is not to be the dominant factor.

Other corporation directors rise differently to the challenge. "We," they observe, "have only a limited knowledge of fine arts and particularly of the more modern applications of Abstractionism. We even have rather old-fashioned taste in poetry; and some of us would trade a large mess of modern literature for a couple of good old-fashioned novels. We don't claim to be authorities so we keep out of this. Consequently our gifts will be directed toward activities in respect of which our judgment may perhaps be useful. We propose therefore to be as generous as we think we properly can to Schools of Engineering, Schools of Medicine, and in larger aspect, to research work in pure science. In recondite fields we prefer to leave the judgments, the choices, and the consequent support to other people." This is generous thinking, and creditable. But it seems that our "City of God" leaves artistic values and the humanities for future reference, and meanwhile emphasizes the solid scientific base. Another choice—perhaps a good one—no one really knows.

(One would like to have a record of the thinking of the great Italian banker, Cosimo de' Medici, in the mid-fifteenth century. His bank and business had come to dominate Florence. He ran the little country, though he assumed no political title. He subsidized art and artists, and supported queer penniless refugees from Byzantium who insisted on copying and translating Greek classics. Did he realize that he was laying one of the foundation piers for the Italian Renaissance, one of the greatest efflorescences of human spirit in the Christian era? He was a reflective man, and he may have speculated on the subject. There are some marked similarities between his situation and that of American business five hundred years later.)

One can carry illustrations still further; the reader can do so for himself. But at the far end of any series of illustrations within this huge plat we are beginning to explore, someone may eventually discern a human being multiplied by many millions, each individual unique, sentient, beset by wonders and doubts, endowed with surprising ability, fraught with surprising fears. The millions of him are, by hypothesis, the inhabitants of this new republic. And never in history has he been willing or been able successfully to live in a city which did not have as its illuminating star something he considered above, beyond, and superior to all material considerations, and most of all, above and beyond himself.

3

In the fifth century A.D. one Augustine, Bishop of Hippo in North Africa, surveyed the wreck of the Roman Empire. It had broken into vast, unstable fragments. The Roman peace and the Roman imperial order had ceased to be the framework with which life could be formed. New institutions were appearing; old ones were breaking up. In the words of the Psalmist, the foundations of the earth were out of course, and whole peoples walked in darkness.

This prelate had had full measure of experience with the phenomena of power. As bishop, he had held some himself. As observer of the ebb of empire and of men who seized kingdoms or forged them, he knew quite well that power was only half the story of human organization. Aside from its ecclesiastical implications his study, *The City of God,* was a striking and simple statement of a hypothesis of political science. Underlying, entering, complementing, ultimately controlling every tangible institutional organization of affairs there was inevitably a moral and philosophical organization which continued from age to age and which ultimately directed power. This philosophical content alone gave permanence to institutions; this philosophical organization survived institutional creation. This Augustine christened "The City of God." Because it worked directly on the minds of men wherever and however placed, it could exact action from them within any framework and thus guide any institution. It is, perhaps, the first great source book for the theory of dichotomy of power which has entered this study from time to time.

We have not, up to the present, been accustomed to think of the modern corporation as an institution at all, let alone a political institution. We have thought of it merely as an enterprise (or perhaps combination of enterprises) within a community. American political thought has been frightened, and corporations them-selves have been frightened, at any suggestion that they might emerge as political institutions in their own and separate right. So we have not been accustomed to place over against each other, as necessarily interrelated facts, the pragmatic concept of the corporation and the phil-osophical concept of the desirable community. Corpo-rate executives rather resent being assimilated to poli-ticians; still more they resent being called to account by philosophers. They belong to one of the few groups in history to which political power came unsought, or at any rate as a by-product rather than a main objective. It is probable that when Mr. Harlow Curtice and Mr. Alfred P. Sloan, Jr., wrote in General Motors Annual Report for 1953, that "with the elimination of controls and with the trend away from a centrally managed economy, industry is possessed of the opportunity to make its maximum contribution to the forward march of our country," they did not think they were talking politics at all. Still less, perhaps, would they consider they had assumed in substantial measure the philosophical burden of judging what is and what should be the "forward march" of a very great country. But they had done just that.

Herein lies, perhaps, the greatest current weakness of the corporate system. In practice, institutional corporations are guided by tiny self-perpetuating oligarchies. These in turn are drawn from and judged by the group opinion of a small fragment of America—its business and financial community. Change of management by contesting for stockholders' votes is extremely rare, and increasingly difficult and expensive to the point of impossibility. The legal presumption in favor of management, and the natural unwillingness of courts to control or reverse management action save in cases of the more elementary types of dishonesty or fraud, leaves management with substantially absolute power. Thus the only real control which guides or limits their economic and social action is the real, though undefined and tacit, philosophy of the men who compose them.

Fifteen hundred years ago, St. Augustine made the same observation concerning the men and groups who achieved power in the fragmented territories of the empire that had once been Rome. But he also knew, as the men in power in his time frequently did not, that whatever institutions they built derived permanence, continuity and significance from the philosophy more than from the power; and he endeavored, in the diffuse scholastic fashion of the time, to set the Christian philosophy over against the contemporary power institutions; and he gave impetus and direction to the whole of the Middle Ages.

The lesson, I think, is as valid for the twentieth as for the fifth century. Capitalism is not a way of life, but a method of achieving economic and social results —a method indeed evolving so rapidly that the capitalism of 1954 has but a bowing acquaintance with that of 1854 and little if any real resemblance to the capitalism of 1804. The institutional corporation collectivized capital, and like most collectivisms concentrated power into a small directing group. The aggregate of such groups—a couple of hundred or so—have proved to be the chief instruments of the twentieth-century revolution in the western world outside the Iron Curtain. As yet the community has not created any acknowledged referent of responsibility, no group from which they take their power mandate or get instructions in dealing with serious streams of events they can and do affect. There is no recognized body of doctrine by which they themselves must test their choice as they act from day to day.

4

To anyone who studies and even remotely begins to apprehend the American corporate system, the implications of the line of thought here sketched have both splendor and terror. The argument just made compels the conclusion that the corporation, almost against its will, has been compelled to assume in appreciable part the role of conscience-carrier of twentieth-century American society. Unlike other great groups which have attempted a major part in this task, the modern corporation has done so without intent to dominate and without clearly defined doctrine. The revolutionists who made the Communist Party in the Soviet Union knew more or less what sort of structure they proposed to build, and had at least a glimmer of theory why they wished that result, ghastly as it seems to American thought. The Catholic Church, in the splendid medieval days when it attempted to construct a supranational society, was tolerably clear in its objectives. Somewhat the same quality appeared in Calvin's attempt to remake Geneva, and was not absent from the British Labour Party's accomplishment of the peaceful revolution in Great Britain along philosophical lines pounded out in the Fabian Club. No one, however, has made a blueprint of the community desired by Standard Oil of New Jersey or by Sears, Roebuck & Company, by the Southern Pacific Railroad, or by Ohio Edison, least of all the corporations themselves.

Yet it seems the aggregate of their day-to-day decisions do form life and community. They do play a notable part in the physical bases on which life is lived. They build or shift or direct frameworks of human experience within which great masses of men live. Indirectly they affect an even greater peripheral group. They do enter into those community institutions, now including colleges and schools and philanthropies, which are the proudest product of American life. To the extent, therefore, that corporation managements, knowingly or unknowingly, reflect a philosophy, they have become a powerful force.

This is a vast and in some ways a humorous historical paradox. Our grandfathers quarreled with corporations because, as the phrase went, they were "soulless." But out of the common denominator of the decision-making machinery, some sort of consensus of mind is emerging, by compulsion as it were, which for good or ill is acting surprisingly like a collective soul. Great organizations energizing this sort of causative apparatus have their frightening side. When Mary Wollstonecraft Shelley's hero, Frankenstein, endowed his synthetic robot with a human heart, the monster which before had been a useful mechanical servant suddenly became an uncontrollable force. Our ancestors feared that corporations had no conscience. We are treated to the colder, more modern fear that, perhaps, they do.

Certain safeguards do exist. Perhaps during the next hitch in this twentieth-century drama they will be sufficient. The great difference between the American corporate system and any socialist system lies in the fact that in America there are a few hundred powerful units, each of which has a limited capacity to disagree with its fellow giants and to do something different. If Professor Adelman of Massachusetts Institute of Technology is right, concentration though great is not increasing rapidly; the writer agrees that it is proceeding slowly, though probably with somewhat greater speed than Adelman's figures disclose.

To begin with, there is a mighty difference between results obtained by the individual action of some hundreds of large units, unencumbered by a central group which proclaims orthodox doctrine and punishes deviation, and results obtained when substantially all determinative units are compelled to a common standard of choice and action by a central committee or by some central dogma. It is said at the moment that the business world places an undue value on conformity; and this is true. But in the not too distant future it may well appear that the men in the corporate world who stand for unpopular doctrine, who insist, for example, on providing scholarships for poets when well-thought-of businessmen only subsidize engineering research, or even men who insist that community formation is for individuals and therefore compel distribution of profits to their shareholders, instead of conscripting part of them for education and charity, may be found to be the true saviors of a free, energetic, and competitive society. As yet the picture of a central group of "interests" capable of enforcing general agreement is a bogeyman set up by demagogues: it does not exist outside of cartoons. The reality—a "conscience" in business organizations which do control many men—need be neither impractical nor dangerous once the business community has learned to honor difference and deviation as well as agreement and conformity. Happily in America there have always been the men who will not "go along." We have reason to hope there will be enough disagreement so that the nuclei of power and of social organization will not only agree, but differ as well.

5

There is also still another and greater hope. Even within the pressures which organizations exact—even in spite of the necessity that men in great enterprises shall work as a team—the individuals themselves are invariably influenced by certain great philosophical premises. These, in our system, are not derived from within business organization. They come from schools and from teachers; from universities and philosophers; from men of deep human instinct who are, by occasional miracle, saints. Their strength comes from instincts and impulses deeper perhaps than any of us understand. If these impulses, as we hope they may, continue to demand the self-realization of individuals, if they continue to call for methods, institutions and remedies making it possible for every man to protect his personality against invasion, then society emerging in the capitalist revolution will continue to be free, just as the democratic system was the work of men of courage, working against the background of feudal dictatorship of seven centuries ago. A director who stoutly says his corporation has no business to tackle the problem of community organization may go farther, and (for example) with equal stoutness refuse to let his publicity people insert propaganda into public schools. The director who, equally stoutly, says his corporation must assure attainable first-rate education may carry his thinking to the point of demanding (as some to their everlasting honor have already done) that academic freedom shall be inviolate, and that controversiality shall be reckoned a virtue, not a fault. In fixing attention on the organization which has been our field of study, one must not forget that the organization itself is composed of men. The common resistance point of these individuals ultimately determines how far any organization can go.

In ascending scale is the fact that so long as speech and thought are free, men will always rise capable of transcending the massed effects of any organization or group of organizations. There is solid ground for the expectation that twenty years from now the men of greatest renown in the United States will be the spiritual, philosophical, and intellectual leaders for the sufficient reason that they will be needed more than any other type of men. Society still tends both to produce and to honor the kinds of men it needs most.

We have noted that priests have usually been able to intimidate the policemen, and that philosophers can usually check the politicians. There is fair historical ground to anticipate that moral and intellectual leadership will appear capable of balancing our Frankenstein creations. Men working in that range are measurably steeled to resist normal pressures and often free from normal fears. They frequently have a rough time on the way. It is no accident that some of the greatest saints in the Christian Calendar were non-conformist deviants in their time; but they still grasp the future with their conceptions.

These, I think, are the real builders of any "City of God" Americans would come to accept. Corporations cannot make them. But they may protect and maintain them. Corporate managements, like others, knowingly or unknowingly, are constrained to work within a frame of surrounding conceptions which in time impose themselves. The price of failure to understand and observe them is decay of the corporation itself. Such conceptions emerge in time as law. It may be said of the corporation as old Bracton said of the Crown: "There is no king where the will and not the law prevails."

BIBLIOGRAPHICAL NOTE

Since these chapters are an essay rather than full-dress academic presentation, the writer has not followed the custom of page by page footnotes and references.

Where published books are referred to in the text, they are readily identifiable in the appended bibliography. In certain respects information not readily available has been drawn on, and acknowledgment should be made here.

The estimate of concentration made by Professor M. A. Adelman of Massachusetts Institute of Technology appears in an article of his, "The Measurement of Industrial Concentration," *The Review of Economics & Statistics*, November, 1951 (Vol. XXXII, No. 4). The estimate appears on page 289; but the whole article is essential to get a statistical picture in which there are still many gaps. Critique of it appears in *The Review of Economics & Statistics*, May, 1952 (Vol. XXXIV, No. 2). For those who are interested in the names of corporations, there is an excellent list of the "100 Largest" in *The National City Monthly Letter on Economic Conditions—Government Finance* for June, 1952.

The private study of the sources of capital made by the writer and Dr. Irvin S. Bussing was privately printed and is not generally available. The conclusions accorded substantially with those expressed by *The National City Monthly Letter on Business and Economic Conditions* for November, 1953. The National City Monthly Letters are available both at the National City Bank, New York City, and at most economic and business libraries.

Professor Kenneth Boulding's book, *The Organizational Revolution* (New York: Harper & Bros., 1953) was one of a series of studies on ethics and economic life, produced by a study committee of the Federal Council of Churches under the Chairmanship of Charles P. Taft.

The data as to the handling of the General Motors agency contracts was collected for the writer by Mr. Charles T. Alberti, then of the Columbia Law School and presently a member of the Massachusetts Bar.

The data as to the European view on cartels was derived from conversations with a number of leading Europeans but chiefly from M. Paul Van Zeeland whose conclusion is worth repeating: "For us, the question is not whether there should be cartels: it is whether they are so operated that their results are good."

The material regarding the successful endeavor made by Mr. Spruille Braden, then Ambassador to Cuba, to head off involvement of American corporations in Cuba in local politics is embodied in a telegram-dispatch from him (at date of sending it he was United States Ambassador to Argentina) to the writer, then United States Ambassador to Brazil; the original is in the State Department files.

The data concerning the price war between the oil companies and the ensuing "Achnacarry Agreement" was collected for the writer by Messrs. Alexander Andrews, Jr. and William Perlmuth, then of the Columbia Law School, and presently members of the New York Bar. Much of this material appears in the Federal Trade Commission Report on *The International Petroleum Cartel* (United States Government Printing Office, Washington, 1952). The oil companies do not accept this presentation, though the writer's impression is that they dispute the interpretation rather than the facts, or perhaps dispute the implication that the situation created by the agreement of September, 1928, prevails today. The industry's comments on the Federal Trade Commission Report unquestionably were conditioned in part by the fact that they were threatened with anti-trust action. They could not therefore assert that the arrangement was a beneficial one, but were forced to assume the position that no cartel arrangement existed.

In other respects it is believed that the text sufficiently indicates the primary and secondary source material.

Of the latter, the interested reader will find a wealth of material in the following books:

Burns, Arthur R., *The Decline of Competition* (New York: McGraw-Hill Company, 1936)

Chamberlin, Edward, *The Theory of Monopolistic Competition* (Cambridge: Harvard University Press, 1933)

Dewhurst, J. Frederic, *America's Needs and Resources* (New York: Twentieth Century Fund, 1947) (revised edition is to appear about December, 1954)

Drucker, Peter F., *Concept of the Corporation* (New York: John Day Company, 1946)

Galbraith, J. Kenneth, *American Capitalism: The Concept of Countervailing Power* (Boston: Houghton Mifflin Company, 195?)

Griffin, Clare E., *Enterprise in a Free Society* (Chicago: Richard D. Irwin, Inc., 1949)

Rostow, W. W., *Dynamics of Soviet Society* (New York: W. W. Norton & Company, 1952)

Smith, Adam, *The Wealth of Nations.* The editions are legion.

Stocking, George W. and Watkins, Myron W., *How Big Is Big Business?* (New York: Twentieth Century Fund, 1937)

Stocking, George W. and Watkins, Myron W., *Monopoly and Free Enterprise* (New York: Twentieth Century Fund, 1951)

Wilcox, Clair, *Competition and Monopoly in American Industry* (Washington, D. C., TNEC Monograph No. 21, 1940)

Woytinsky, W. S. and E. S., *World Population and Production* (New York: Twentieth Century Fund, 1953)

70
71
72
74
75
76
77
79
8
83
85
88